PUBLIC FINANCING FOR SMALL AND MEDIUM-SIZED ENTERPRISES

THE CASES OF THE REPUBLIC OF KOREA AND THE UNITED STATES

NOVEMBER 2023

ASIAN DEVELOPMENT BANK

 Creative Commons Attribution 3.0 IGO license (CC BY 3.0 IGO)

Notes:
In this publication, "$" refers to United States dollars.
ADB recognizes "Korea" as the Republic of Korea.

Cover design by Anthony Villanueva.

On the cover: Small and medium-sized enterprises in Asia contribute significantly to economic development and
employment, yet face difficulties accessing finance. (photo by ADB).

Contents

Tables, Figures, and Boxes

Boxes

Foreword

Robust economic growth in recent years has alleviated poverty and added to the number of middle-income countries in the world. Economies had to evolve, however, to overcome slowdowns brought about by several financial crises and the coronavirus disease (COVID-19) pandemic and to strengthen small and medium-sized enterprises (SMEs) and thus boost national productivity. Small firms, often hardest hit during economic turmoil, account for the majority of businesses worldwide and are important contributors to job creation and global economic development, particularly in the developing world.

In Asia alone, SMEs are considered the backbone of their respective economies. A 2016 report by the Asian Development Bank Institute (ADBI) reveals that SMEs make up more than 98% of all Asian businesses and provide two of three private sector jobs. Clearly, this calls for fully functioning support measures for SMEs, which need financing, particularly in investment (machinery, production sites, and others), working capital (stocks, factors of production, current operating outlays, and others), or both.

Yet, SMEs face major obstacles to access finance to grow their businesses in emerging markets and developing countries. They are less likely than firms to obtain bank loans and, instead, rely on internal funds or cash from friends and family to launch and initially run their enterprises. This is because banks prefer to allocate their resources to large enterprises rather than to SMEs. The same 2016 ADBI report says this is because large enterprises have a lower risk of default and their financial statements are clear. Lenders thus see SMEs as riskier and doubt their ability to repay financing, as they often do not have clear accounting information. Although SME access to bank finance largely recovered after the global financial crisis, long-standing challenges remain, such as information asymmetries, high transaction costs, and lack of financial skills and knowledge among small business owners. Financing instruments other than straight debt often remain underdeveloped. And micro-enterprises, innovative ventures, start-ups (except high-potential start-ups), and young firms thus tend to face more difficulties in accessing finance.

Policymakers play a significant role in overcoming the impediments to SME access to credit. This study provides potential policy solutions implemented in the Republic of Korea and the United States (US). Governments can set up specialized banks to provide credit to SMEs, for example, such as the Republic of Korea's establishment of the Industrial Bank of Korea (IBK). Another policy may involve setting up government entities to provide loans and guarantees to SMEs that apply for credit from traditional financial institutions, such as commercial banks. This was applied in the creation of the U.S. Small Business Administration (SBA) in the United States.

The cases outlined in this report can help economies in Asia and the Pacific develop and warrant careful consideration, with their focus on financial products, risk management, monitoring methodologies, and nonfinancial services for SMEs. Indeed, countries around the world should consider following the lead of the US and the Republic of Korea in establishing public lending schemes to support small-business revenues and growth, using their IBK and SBA as templates. We are confident policymakers will find this study useful.

Ramesh Subramaniam
Director General and Group Chief Sectors Group
Asian Development Bank

Acknowledgments

The technical study, Public Financing for Small and Medium-Sized Enterprises: The Cases of the Republic of Korea and the United States, is a product of the Sector Group of the Asian Development Bank (ADB). The study is part of a series in the ADB Finance Sector Office's SME financing knowledge products, which aim to support efforts to expand SME financing in developing member countries in Asia and the Pacific.

Junkyu Lee, director, Finance Sector Office, Sectors Group, ADB provided key inputs and led a core team in preparing the technical study. Sung Su Kim, senior financial sector specialist (inclusive finance), Finance Sector Office, Sectors Group, ADB coordinated and contributed to production, with technical inputs from Rebel Cole, professor, Florida Atlantic University, and Jae-Joon Han, professor, Inha University. Raquel Borres, Katherine Mitzi Co, Matilde Mila Cauinian, Mary Anndie Clavel, and Mc Reynald II Banderlipe provided technical and research support. In particular, the team expresses its gratitude to the Industrial Bank of Korea for reviewing this technical study and providing practical information.

The team thanks Yuji Miyaki, public management specialist (taxation), Public Sector Management and Governance Sector Office, Sectors Group, ADB, who played a peer reviewer role and Manohari Gunawardhena, senior financial sector specialist Finance Sector Office, Sectors Group, ADB, and Damitha Kumari Rathnayake, chief executive officer, Regional Development Bank in Sri Lanka, who gave presentations at the webinar on 25 February 2021 and made suggestions for developing the report.

The team greatly appreciates Ramesh Subramaniam, director general and group chief, Sectors Group; Sungsup Ra, deputy director general and deputy group chief, Sectors Group; and Christine Engstrom, senior director Finance Sector Office, Sectors Group, for their proactive support for the knowledge events and the report.

We thank all contributors for their generous efforts on this publication and the team also acknowledges colleagues from the Department of Communications and Knowledge Management for their continuous support in disseminating the report.

Abbreviations

ADB	Asian Development Bank
CARES	Coronavirus Aid, Relief, and Economic Security
EIDL	economic-injury disaster loans
FTP	fast-track program
FY	fiscal year
GDP	gross domestic product
IBK	Industrial Bank of Korea
KODIT	Korea Credit Guarantee Fund
MSMEs	micro, small, and medium-sized enterprises
SBA	small business administration
SBIC	small business investment company
SMEs	small and medium-sized enterprises
SMIF	small and medium industry finance bonds
US	United States

Executive Summary

Small and medium-sized enterprises (SMEs) are widely considered the backbone of economies through their contribution to economic growth and employment. "Formal" SMEs account for more than 90% of all firms and for more than half of employment around the world (World Bank n.d.). Yet, access to finance is a key constraint for SMEs in growing their businesses in emerging and developed economies (World Bank n.d.). These small firms have limited access to capital markets and difficulty obtaining formal finance from lenders such as commercial banks. Several factors hinder SME access to formal finance. These include asymmetric information, in which limited public information about SMEs discourages lenders, and financial regulations that require due diligence in underwriting credit. They also include lack of tangible assets of SMEs to meet collateral requirements, poor financial records and statements of SMEs, and lack of credit-reporting institutions and capacity of such institutions to help lenders accurately assess the risk of SMEs. Therefore, SMEs usually obtain financing from informal finance or funding from sources unregulated by financial supervisors, which thus includes not only professional money lenders, but also trade credit from other enterprises and loans from friends and family. As such, when SMEs can obtain formal finance, they often face onerous loan terms, including short-term tenor, high interest rates, and demand for collateral.

To overcome the impediments to SME access to credit, nonetheless, policymakers have a few potential solutions. Governments can set up specialized banks to provide credit to SMEs, for example, as the Republic of Korea did with the Industrial Bank of Korea. They can also set up government entities to provide loan guarantees to SMEs that apply for credit from traditional financial institutions, such as commercial banks. The U.S. Small Business Administration (SBA) is one such organization. This report details how these two specific cases of public SME financing have helped improve SMEs' access to credit. These cases are useful to policymakers in other countries in tackling the access issue.

Republic of Korea

SMEs in the Republic of Korea have received strong public policy support for the past 50 years, regardless of changes in government or economic policy. The Ministry of SMEs and Startups is mandated to develop and implement government policy for promoting business growth, fostering start-ups, and supporting micro, small, and medium-sized enterprises. The ministry collaborates with nine SME-related (or affiliated) institutions to provide financial, marketing, and technological support. Among them are the Industrial Bank of Korea (IBK) for financing, the Korea Credit Guarantee Fund for credit guarantee services, the Korea Technology Finance Corporation for technology financing, and the Korea SMEs and Startups Agency.[1]

---

[1]   See Ministry of SMEs and Startups at https://www.mss.go.kr/site/eng/01/20104000000002019110651.jsp.

IBK was established in 1961 as a public bank under the Industrial Bank of Korea Act to provide financial services to SMEs whose access to market resources was limited and constrained, with the act designed to facilitate IBK's outreach. It is required to allocate at least 70% of its loan portfolio to SMEs. The Government of the Republic of Korea also enables IBK to issue Small and Medium Industry Finance bonds separately—with a government guarantee of the interest and principal repayment—to prepare loan resources, because deposits alone are not enough for IBK to raise the funds it needs. Since 1981, IBK has provided policy loans to SMEs making various intermediate goods—such as diverse parts, industrial materials, or tools—and selling them to big firms. In 1989, IBK expanded the scope of its SME policy loan provision to small firms with good potential for growth and with employees numbering fewer than 50. Since 1991, IBK has enabled lending within certain limits without the need for physical collateral or a joint guarantor, greatly contributing to lower financial costs and simplifying lending procedures. IBK provides consulting support to SMEs at every stage of business, as well as financing.

In addition, lending directly to SMEs, IBK served as an agency to provide credit guarantees for small business loans.[2] It established the Credit Guarantee Fund in 1967 with credit guarantee reserves and government contributions and guarantee fees. And as the subject and role of the Credit Guarantee Fund expanded, the Korean government separated its functions from IBK in 1976 and established a separate organization called the Korea Credit Guarantee Fund, which has been performing well so far.

IBK later began expanding its nonbanking financial business through acquisitions and new establishments, starting with the establishment of a Korean corporate lease in 1986 to overcome the limitations of financial support for SMEs through loans. It also provides nonbank financial services through securities companies, venture capital, capital companies, asset management companies, and credit information companies, in addition to banks dedicated to SMEs. Through the participation of these IBK Financial Group constituents, IBK offers comprehensive support measures such as recruitment of investors for SMEs, equity investment decisions, investment and technical advice, and credit reinforcement and facility lending, in addition to loans. IBK itself also provides consulting support to SMEs at every stage of business, in addition to financing. Even though IBK's business is limited only to SMEs, it has generated favorable earnings and has induced the participation of commercial banks to the SME financing market. As of 2018, the size of IBK's SME loan portfolio was $124 billion, which includes $35 billion in lending to micro-businesses.

United States

In the United States (US), meanwhile, the SBA was created and established by the Small Business Act of 1953 as an independent agency dedicated to aiding, counseling, assisting, and protecting the interests of small business concerns. This includes the protection of small business rights in getting a fair proportion of government contracts and sales of surplus property.[3] The SBA's mission is to "maintain and strengthen the nation's economy by enabling the establishment and vitality of small businesses and by assisting in the economic recovery of communities after disasters."

---

[2] A credit guarantee is a legal contract by which a third party, known as the guarantor, promises to repay part or all of the amount of a loan to a lender should the borrower default.
[3] Small Business Act (Public Law 85–536, as amended).

The SBA administers different programs to support small businesses of the US economy. These include loan-guarantee programs designed to increase access to private-sector debt and venture capital programs designed to increase access to private-sector equity. It also includes contracting programs to improve access to federal contracts; direct lending programs to assist businesses, homeowners, and renters in recovering from disasters triggered by natural hazards; and training programs to assist in business formation and expansion (Congressional Research Service 2019).

The SBA's flagship is its 7(a) loan-guarantee program, which is generally used for businesses to meet various needs, such as equipment purchases, working capital, leasehold improvements, inventory, or real estate purchases. The standard 7(a) program provides a 75%–85% guarantee for SME loans up to $5 million.

The SBA also operates the innovative Small Business Investment Company Program, which, through a public–private partnership, brings the "full faith" and credit of the Government of the United States to boost private-sector investment capital available to small firms. The SBA raises capital by issuing taxpayer-backed debentures guaranteed by the SBA and then combines these funds with capital raised by privately and publicly managed investment funds that raise capital from private investors, such as banks, pension funds, or wealthy individuals.

These two specific cases of public institutional approaches, the Korean and US, have a strong track record of improving access to credit. This technical study outlines their experiences, which can guide policymakers in developing member countries in Asia as they tackle the SMEs' financial access.

I Introduction

This study discusses small and medium-sized enterprises (SMEs) in detail, including the challenges in financing these entities. Even though they are the backbone of economies through their contribution to economic growth and employment, SMEs still face enormous challenges to expand their businesses. They have limited access to capital markets and difficulty obtaining formal finance. One might wonder what factors hinder and discourage SMEs from accessing formal finance. And given these hindrances, where do they usually obtain financing and does limited access bring challenges to SMEs' growth and sustainability?

It is crucial to understand the economic contribution of SMEs, particularly to employment. Given their role in reducing poverty and inequality, attention should be paid to providing an enabling environment for SMEs to obtain financing. At present, SMEs face internal and external barriers to accessing financial resources. With the current asset-based lending principle and practices, SMEs are deemed risky and expensive businesses to deal with.

Banking systems are being supported to become stronger institutions and more resilient in dealing with operational and credit risks. Through the international banking standards set by the Basel Committee on Banking Supervision, its second installment of standards known as Basel II, provides guidance on extending retail credit and loans given their lower sensitivity to systematic and default risks. The peculiarities of risks are why Basel II encourages differential treatment on retail credit. This implies that the banks' capitalization requirements must be aligned with the creditworthiness of SMEs to enable the infusion of additional capital.

In the aftermath of the global financial crisis of 2008, the committee developed Basel III to strengthen regulation, supervision, and risk management within the banking industry beyond Basel II. This new accord prevents banking institutions from causing more harm by assuming greater risk beyond their capacity. The reforms raise questions regarding short-run costs that SMEs will incur associated with the new regulation. Since most SMEs derive their financing from banks, will such a mechanism affect SMEs' access to financing for their growth?

It is also imperative to underscore the adverse impacts of both Basel II and Basel III on SME lending, as well as the initiatives that regulators seek to put in place to aid and ease the financing of SMEs. Reducing such risks will enable these institutions to position themselves as strong candidates for obtaining formal financing.

Following this detailed discourse on the challenges of SME financing, this technical study directs our attention to the cases of SME lending and support systems in two countries: the Republic of Korea and the United States of America. These two countries provided strong case studies on how governments set up specialized public institutions to provide credit to SMEs, as well as entities that provide loan guarantees to SMEs that apply for credit from traditional financial institutions. A detailed presentation in this study highlights the initiatives of government institutions in these two countries to improve access to credit.

The remaining parts of the study are presented as follows: Section II reviews SMEs and the present-day challenges of SME financing, including those financing from external sources. Section III underscores specific provisions from both Basel II and Basel III and their impacts on SMEs. Section IV presents SME public lending in the case of the Industrial Bank of Korea (IBK), while Section V highlights the case of SME financial support through the U.S. Small Business Administration (SBA). Section VI concludes.

Definition of a Small and Medium-Sized Enterprise

"Small and medium-sized enterprise," simply enough, refers to all firms not "large" in size. Size can be defined by several metrics, however, including total assets, annual sales revenues, and the number of employees. Various thresholds for each measure are used to separate SMEs from large firms, but assets and revenues are country-specific.

Employment is the most common metric in determining SME size, as this metric allows ready comparison across countries without regard to currency or levels. That said, even using employment, the definition of an SME varies from country to country and even within a country from one source to another and, in some countries, from one industry to another. However, many sources exist around the world that use 250 employees as the delineation between an SME and a large enterprise. According to the World Bank, small enterprises have less than 50 employees, while medium-sized enterprises have 50–249 employees.[4]

Formal and informal enterprises can also be distinguished. Formal enterprises must register with the government while informal enterprises do not register. In general, SMEs are defined as formal enterprises, but, in many countries, including the US, sole proprietorships are not required to register, even though these firms are usually counted as formal.

The Economic Contribution of Small and Medium-Sized Enterprises

SMEs constitute the backbone of economies around the globe through their contribution to growth and employment. A survey of prominent Asian countries from 5 regions shows that SMEs account for 96% of all enterprises and employ 62% of their workforce.[5] In addition, they contribute 42% of gross domestic product (GDP) or manufacturing value-added, on average.

---

[4] World Bank. Micro, Small and Medium Enterprises (Number). https://datacatalog.worldbank.org/micro-small-and-medium-enterprises-number (accessed 22 November 2020).

[5] The countries are Bangladesh, Cambodia, People's Republic of China, Fiji, India, Indonesia, Kazakhstan, Republic of Korea, Kyrgyz Republic, Lao People's Democratic Republic (Lao PDR), Malaysia, Mongolia, Papua New Guinea, Philippines, Solomon Islands, Sri Lanka, Tajikistan, Thailand, Viet Nam. See ADB (2015).

In the United States, as per the fiscal year (FY) 2022 Annual Performance Report, the U.S. SBA has worked to equip the country`s nearly 33 million small businesses and innovative start-ups, delivering two-thirds of net new jobs, employing nearly half of the private sector workforce, and producing 40% of the nation`s economic output.[6] The World Bank estimates that formal SMEs constitute more than 90% of all businesses and account for more than half of employment generated across the world (World Bank n.d.). And in emerging economies, it says, SMEs account for up to 40% of GDP and for about 70% of new job creation. The World Trade Organization (WTO) reports that SMEs in developed countries are important vehicles for reducing poverty and for increasing the financial inclusion of women and minorities (WTO 2016), but notes that SMEs are less productive than larger firms, leading to higher failure rates. SMEs account for only about one-third of exports, and this share is much smaller in developing economies—in the range of less than 10% (WTO 2016). It cautions nonetheless that information about exports by SMEs in developing countries is often unreliable because data is simply not available.

Problems for Small and Medium-Sized Enterprises in Obtaining Access to Credit

Despite the great efforts made, lack of access to credit is still a major hindrance faced by firms, especially the SMEs, that reduces their contribution to economic growth (Beck and Demirguc-Kunt 2006; Beck, Demirguc-Kunt, and Maksimovic 2005). SMEs face major challenges in accessing credit, mainly because of the asymmetric information problem between suppliers and demanders of funds and the high transaction costs (ADBI 2018). These constraints lead to more collateral requirements for lending to SMEs and higher lending interest rates. As a result, these hinder business and economic growth. The International Finance Corporation estimates that two in five SMEs—65 million enterprises—in developing countries have unmet financing needs of $5.2 trillion per year, which is about 140% of current lending to such firms.[7] A survey that the ADB Asia SME Finance Monitor carried out on 20 countries from 5 ADB regions highlighted that limited access to bank credit is a structural problem in the monitor's region.[8] Bank loans to SMEs make up averages of 11.6% of GDP and 18.7% of total bank lending in the region, with the latter trending lower since the 2008/09 global financial crisis. Comparing SME access to bank credit relative to the income level of the countries in which they operate, bank credit reaches out to a larger number of SMEs (with a relatively low ratio of nonperforming loans) as the country's economy becomes more advanced (ADB 2015).

---

[6]   Overview of FY 2024 Budget Request and Performance Plan, FY 2024 Congressional Budget Justification, FY 2022 Annual Performance Report.

[7]   In a study of access to credit in 118 countries around the world using World Bank Enterprise Survey data, Cole, Dietrich, and Frost (2019) find that more than half of SMEs reporting a need for credit also reported that they were discouraged and did not apply; of the remaining firms that did apply, about 29% were denied. Together, discouraged and denied firms accounted for roughly two-thirds of all SMEs reporting a need for credit.

[8]   ADB Asia SME Finance Monitor. Countries include- (i) Kazakhstan, the Kyrgyz Republic, and Tajikistan in Central Asia; (ii) the People's Republic of China, the Republic of Korea, and Mongolia in East Asia; (iii) Bangladesh, India, and Sri Lanka in South Asia; (iv) Cambodia, Indonesia, Lao PDR, Malaysia, the Philippines, Thailand, and Viet Nam in Southeast Asia; and (v) Papua New Guinea, Fiji, and the Solomon Islands in the Pacific.

Furthermore, both internal and external factors restrict access to financial resources in developing countries. Internally, most SMEs are uncreditworthy and lack management skills, which makes it difficult for them to obtain funding for essential business activities such as buying raw materials and finished goods, and making investments in machinery and equipment. Because they lack collateral and can only receive a limited amount of funding from financial institutions, SMEs are seen as risky and expensive businesses to deal with. As a result, they have limited access to credit due to high intermediary costs, such as the cost of monitoring and challenges enforcing loan agreements (UNCTAD 2002).

Limited access to capital markets. Because of their size, only a tiny fraction of SMEs has access to either debt or equity capital markets. Capital markets are a popular financing source for large companies and an alternative to bank loans for SMEs, but only 25% of SMEs use equity financing as their primary way to raise money, according to an International Organization of Securities Commissions study. Fear of losing ownership of the business, relatively high regulatory costs, and inexperience with capital markets tend to discourage SMEs from accessing capital markets. Venture capital and angel investing have been providing new financing opportunities for innovative, high-growth potential start-ups (mainly SMEs) in financial technology (fintech) fields. These are usually accessed by SMEs through fintech companies or online lending platforms. The online lending market has continued to evolve and expand, particularly during the pandemic. According to a recent report by the Cambridge Centre for Alternative Finance, online alternative finance platforms in the United States facilitated more than $15 billion of loans to small and medium enterprises in 2019 (Ziegler et al. 2021). While this amount remains small relative to the small business credit market as a whole—for reference, outstanding small loans to businesses on bank balance sheets in 2019, quarter 4 was $607 billion—this market has grown rapidly from less than $10 billion in 2016 (Federal Reserve 2022).

Informational asymmetries. Asymmetric information is a fundamental problem for SMEs. This is when one of two parties in an economic transaction has more accurate information than the other. In the case of a borrower and a lender, the lender has less accurate information about the true financial condition of the borrower than does the borrower (Stiglitz and Weiss 1981; Diamond 1984). This gives rise to "adverse selection," in that a less-creditworthy borrower is more likely to apply for credit from the lender who is then more likely to offer the credit at a higher rate or likely to decline the credit for SMEs. Asymmetric information is mitigated when there is more publicly available information about the borrower. But for SMEs, especially young SMEs, little public information is available, giving lenders an incentive to avoid lending to these firms unless they can provide collateral and/or audited financial statements.

Financial regulation. Financial institutions must comply with regulations that require them to exercise due diligence in underwriting credit, even small-denomination loans to SMEs. For example, under anti-money-laundering regulations, they must investigate new customers to ensure they are not dealing with customers engaged in illegal activities. This increases the fixed costs of loan originations, which often make small-denomination loans to SMEs unprofitable for regulated financial institutions.

Collateral requirements. Loan-underwriting practices typically require collateral provision by SME borrowers. Collateral can be of many forms, including cash bank deposits, but usually tangible real assets such as equipment or real property (land and buildings). But most SMEs, especially at the inception stage, have few tangible assets to meet collateral requirements and are thus unable to obtain credit from financial institutions. Calomiris et al. (2017) study the distinction between movable collateral (e.g., accounts receivable, inventory, machinery, and vehicles) and immovable collateral (e.g., real property [buildings and land]). Collateral laws for movable assets are much weaker in developing countries than in developed countries. The authors find that borrowers obtain significantly higher loan-to-value ratios in countries with stronger protection of creditors' rights to seize movable collateral. In other words, a borrower can obtain more credit when pledging the same amount of collateral in countries that better protect creditor rights to seize movable collateral.

Financial record requirements. Sound loan-underwriting practices require financial institutions to ask borrowers for financial records and financial statements, including balance sheets and profit-and-loss statements. Many lenders will ask for audited financial statements, especially for larger loan requests. However, most SMEs are not legally required to prepare such financial statements. They are unlikely to willingly pay for a formal audit of finances and thus may have only poor financial records to underpin their financial statements. In the area of controlled accounting, about 72% of participants prepare a financial statement at least annually: 49% of respondents include a balance sheet, an income statement, a statement of change in equity, and a cash flow; and 23% of financial statements do not contain these four reports (one, two, or three), and only 14% of SMEs have an external auditor prepare, check, and certify their financial statements (World Bank 2018). This is especially true in developing countries, where computerized records are often not available. In this situation, SMEs are unlikely to obtain credit from financial institutions.

Strengthening accounting and auditing is thus a prerequisite for SMEs to gain access to banks. With audited financial statements, reducing information risk, and improving borrower credibility, lending institutions may offer credit services to SMEs with lower interest rates and longer tenor. Therefore, it is crucial that reputable credit bureaus and financial databases be established, coupled with the borrower's capability to submit sufficient financial statements to support the expansion of credit, foster competition in banking systems, and thereby lower borrowers' credit costs.

Excessive requirements for collateral and guarantees. SMEs' insufficient collateral and the higher interest rates are major hindrances to SME credit access. As noted, excessive collateral and guarantee requirements exist, while banks impose unreasonably high lending rates on SME borrowers, resulting in supply-side impediments that are likely to hinder SME growth. In many cases, SMEs cannot access loans from financial institutions because of harsher requirements. Financial institutions refuse to lend to some small enterprises with insufficient collateral since tangible asset collateral is one way they can recover their money in case of default. Otherwise, banks have limited recourse for recovering funds.

Financial illiteracy. Financial illiteracy, a major problem and a key reason SMEs are unable to access loans, is the inability to understand basic financial concepts, such as budgeting, the time value of money, financial statements, or how a creditor evaluates a loan application. Cole, Dietrich, and Frost (2019) find that almost four times as many firms do not apply for credit—as do apply and are turned down—when they need it because they fear rejection. They estimate that at least one-third of these "discouraged" firms would have received credit, if only they had applied. They attribute this, in large part, to the financial illiteracy of the discouraged borrowers.

The majority of SMEs are unable to grasp the extensive terms and conditions of a commercial loan. Microfinance organizations are seen as performing a valuable service by providing credit facilities for SMEs, but they do not always convey the truth. Some of these institutions take advantage of the borrowers' lack of education and fail to provide specifics and explain the interest rates and their ramifications for the small borrower, for various reasons. This leads to a problem when those borrowers cannot meet the loan repayment terms.

Small enterprises often do not know what factors financial institutions consider when evaluating a commercial credit application. Because lending to companies ready to pay higher interest rates would attract riskier borrowers, financial institutions normally do not lend to them, i.e., adverse selection. Lenders have methods for checking the creditworthiness of their potential borrowers. As such, this lack of understanding of banks' underwriting procedures is a key factor behind SMEs' inability to access financial assistance. They consequently suffer frustrating delays in accessing bank credit or outright credit denial. As noted, banks demand documentation, such as audited financial information, convincing business plans, and bankable proposals before they will lend to a small business. Yet, most small enterprises lack the technical capacity to provide such documentation, complicating their credit access.

Policymakers and program providers, therefore, emphasize key lessons that can improve current and develop future financial education policies and initiatives to enhance the financial literacy of micro, small, and medium-sized enterprises (MSMEs) and potential entrepreneurs. These include:

(i)　conducting frequent, rigorous surveys to gauge the financial literacy of MSMEs and aspiring business owners and to offer deeper insights into the financial literacy levels of various groups operating in the MSME sector;

(ii)　designing programs specific to target groups and accounting for macro and micro levels for the MSME sector;

(iii)　concentrating on developing business-specific competencies that aim to improve both general and business-specific literacy;

(iv)　giving owners personalized guidance and mentoring from professionals to introduce them to relatable local role models and success stories;

(v)　expanding the selection of delivery methods to increase the range of resources available to entrepreneurs;

(vi)　locating prospective entrepreneurs outside of the educational system to encourage a high level of entrepreneurial activity;

(vii)　increasing the financial sector's participation in financial education; and

(viii)　regularizing the assessment of financial literacy initiatives to identify their efficacy and potential for development (OECD 2017).

Banks impose high lending rates on SME borrowers. When a formal lender such as a commercial bank underwrites a loan, it incurs significant costs. These include costs associated with "onboarding" a new customer; assessing the risk of default by the borrower; calculating loss, given default; and, if the bank extends credit, the cost of processing the loan and then monitoring the borrower until it is fully repaid. These procedures are expensive, even for small-denomination loans, so lenders pass the costs on to borrowers, usually in the form of higher lending rates for smaller loans.

However, small-business owners often are not transparent and do not want to share financial information with outsiders. For whatever reason, they may not provide true information about the value of their assets, liabilities, revenues, and profits to tax collectors, their employees, or outsiders. This makes it challenging for small entrepreneurs to assess credit services and for financial institutions to lend to them. Conversely, accurate financial information facilitates assessment of the creditworthiness of enterprises and reduces both the probability of default and expected loss given default. This enables financial institutions to offer better terms of credit to more transparent SMEs. The ability to get external financing is contingent on an open exchange of information between the borrower and the lender. More openness and improved communication between SMEs and financial institutions reduce the difficulty of obtaining loans.

After a lender extends credit to an SME, it must still consume time and resources to assess, monitor, and manage the credit facility, an expensive business, as noted. Many bankers believe that a small firm requires much more advisory support than does a large corporate client. Again, the lender is likely to pass these costs on to borrowers as fees or higher loan rates. Furthermore, many of these costs are fixed and are not a function of the size of the loan and, consequently, these fixed underwriting costs are proportionately larger for smaller loans.

This leaves the banker with two options for small-denomination loans to MSMEs. The first is to simply ration credit by refusing to underwrite loans below some minimal monetary threshold or other criteria, such as collateral or guarantees. The second is to offer credit to even very small firms, but to charge a higher interest rate on small-denomination loans that is sufficient to cover the fixed underwriting costs.

Different financial institutions in different jurisdictions choose different options. Large institutions are more likely to ration credit and simply abandon the small-loan market. Smaller institutions are more likely to choose to offer credit in the small-loan market, but charge a higher rate than they charge on larger loans. However, in many jurisdictions, lenders face regulatory maximums on loan rates. When faced with a binding lending rate constraint, lenders will simply refuse to underwrite small, unprofitable loans.

How Basel II Affects Small and Medium-Sized Enterprise Financing

Basel II is the Basel Committee on Banking Supervision's second set of international banking standards. It expands Basel I standards on minimum capital requirements. Three pillars serve as the foundation of the Basel II framework. Pillar 1 focuses on capital adequacy requirements and seeks to improve on the policies of Basel I by considering operational risks in addition to credit risks associated with risk-weighted assets. Pillar 1 mandates banks to maintain a minimum capital adequacy requirement of 8% of their risk-weighted assets. Basel II also gives banks better methods for determining their capital adequacy ratio based on the credit risk of their assets, considering the specific characteristics and the risk profile of each asset.

Pillar 2 is concerned with supervisory review and was included to address the lack of supervisory provisions on bank internal capital adequacy under Basel 1. Under Pillar 2, banks are obligated to assess the internal capital adequacy necessary to cover all risks posed by the bank's daily operations. Supervisors are in charge of ensuring that the bank employs suitable risk assessment techniques and covers all related risks. Pillar 3 imposes market discipline provisions through the implementation of mandatory disclosure of relevant market information. Through Pillar 3, market discipline is ensured as relevant financial information is received by its key users.

Basel II's main goal was to make banking systems safer and stable by providing a framework for banks to manage risks more effectively, even during the financial crisis. Basel II adopted a method for calculating capital adequacy ratios that took into account charges for both operational and credit risk. There were also suggestions for a stricter supervisory review procedure and higher standards of market discipline.

Impact of Basel II on SMEs. Basel II has the special features of treating retail credit and loans to SMEs differently than corporate loans and requiring less regulatory capital for given default probabilities. Small business loans and retail credit are generally found to be less sensitive to systematic risk, which is the main justification for this differential treatment. When compared to corporate loans, their default risk is thought to be more idiosyncratic, and as a result, default probabilities are thought to be less correlated. The Basel Committee's technical presumption that maturities are shorter is another factor contributing to the preferential treatment of retail credit (Roszbach 2005).

During consultations for Basel II, a few empirical studies found that the more risk-sensitive nature of Basel II would significantly raise the cost and decrease the availability of finance for SMEs because risk-based capital ratios would require higher capital adequacy ratios and operating profits.[9] In response, the Basel Committee reflected specific changes in the final version to accommodate SME finance. These include (i) allowing banking institutions to utilize the internal ratings-based approach to decrease the capital requirements on SME exposures, (ii) establishing specific risk weight curves for SME exposures, (iii) reducing non-mortgage retail risk exposures, and (iv) recognizing credit risk mitigants such as collateral and guarantees better. These changes successfully addressed the major impact issues of Basel II on SME finance. In line with this, the impact analysis of the Basel Committee suggested that capital requirements for SMEs would not be significantly higher than those under Basel I.[10] Basel II has broader implications for banking stability, SME credit policy, and SME access to credit. Aligning a bank's capital requirements with its borrower's creditworthiness is needed to reduce the risks to banks and the need for additional capital.[11] To improve the enterprise's creditworthiness, SMEs would need to submit well-structured and timely financial statements, maintain their bank accounts in compliance with their loan covenants, disclose any changes in employees and capital engaged in the firm, offer adequate collateral and guarantees, and carefully manage their credit function. Hence, banks will make lending choices based on the risk quality and the capacity to repay loans over time.[12]

How Basel III Affects Small and Medium-Sized Enterprise Financing

The Basel Committee on Banking Supervision developed the Basel III accord to strengthen regulation, supervision, and risk management within the banking industry beyond Basel II. Basel III aims to enhance banks' ability to absorb shocks from financial stress and boost their transparency and disclosure in the aftermath of the global financial crisis of 2008. Basel III builds on the earlier accords, Basel I and II, and is part of a broader effort to improve banking regulation. The agreement attempts to keep banks from causing economic harm by taking on more risk than they can handle. It operates under three pillars focusing on minimum capital requirements, leverage ratios, and liquidity requirements.

Pillar 1 tackles minimum capital requirements. The Basel III accord increased minimum capital requirements for banks from 2% in Basel II to 4.5%, and an additional 2.5% buffer capital requirement brings the total minimum requirement to 7%.[13] Banks can use the buffer when confronted with financial stress, but doing so can lead to even more financial constraints when it comes to dividend payments. As of 2015, the Tier 1 capital requirement increased from Basel II's 4% to Basel III's 6%, which consists of 4.5% of Common Equity Tier 1 and an extra 1.5% of additional Tier 1 capital.[14]

---

9   The ratio is a measurement of a bank's available capital expressed as a percentage of its risk-weighted credit exposure. The capital adequacy ratio is used to protect depositors and promote the stability and efficiency of financial systems around the world. Two types of capital are measured: Tier 1 capital is the primary funding source of the bank. Tier 1 capital consists of shareholders' equity and retained earnings. Tier 2 capital includes revaluation reserves, hybrid capital instruments and subordinated term debt, general loan-loss reserves, and undisclosed reserves.

10   Please see International Finance Corporation for more information at https://www.ifc.org/wps/wcm/connect/dd44ba10-4469-4054-ac68-5dccc1a335ac/G20_Policy_Report.pdf?MOD=AJPERES&CVID=jkWST-A.

11   See Caruana (2003) for more information.

12   See Ayadi (2005) for more information.

13   Measured as a percentage of common equity over the bank's risk-weighted assets.

14   Tier-1 capital is capital that can absorb losses without a bank being required to cease trading.

Pillar 2 is concerned with the leverage ratio. Basel III introduced a non-risk-based leverage ratio as a backstop to the risk-based capital requirements.[15] The non-risk-based leverage ratio is calculated by dividing Tier 1 capital by the average total consolidated assets of a bank. Currently, banks are required to maintain a leverage ratio over 3%.

Pillar 3 focuses on liquidity requirements. Basel III imposed additional regulatory requirements based on two new liquidity ratios—the liquidity coverage ratio and the net stable funding ratio. The liquidity coverage ratio requires that banks retain enough highly liquid assets that can withstand a 30-day stressed funding scenario, as defined by the supervisors. The liquidity coverage ratio mandate was implemented in 2015 at only 60% of its stated requirements and is anticipated to grow 10% a year.

Bond market operations will be impacted by the adoption of these new liquidity rules. Demand for lower-quality corporate bonds will decline because the liquidity coverage ratio requires banks to keep high-quality risk-free assets such as government bonds and covered bonds. As a result, banks will hold more such assets and raise the portfolio proportion of long-term debt to total debt to reduce maturity mismatch to maintain at least the minimum net stable funding ratio. Additionally, banks will scale back businesses that are more vulnerable to liquidity issues. Table 1 summarizes key features of the Basel Accords.

Table 1: Key Features of the Basel Accords

	BASEL I	BASEL II	BASEL III
Purpose	• Contained a set of minimum capital requirements for banks	• "3 pillars" concept introduced • More risk-sensitive	• Created in response to the global financial crisis

Main area of focus	• Credit risk (default risk)
	• Risk-weighting of assets introduced by creating the classification system grouped a bank's assets into five risk categories:
		• Minimum capital requirements (for credit, market, operation)
		• Supervisory review
		• Market discipline (based on market disclosure)
		• Calculation of minimum capital requirements:
		• The standardized approach
		• The internal rating-based approach
		• Securitization framework
		• Operational risk
		• Trading book issues
			• Credit risk
			• Market risk
			• Operational risk
			• Liquidity risk
			   –Two new liquidity ratios:
			      • Liquidity coverage ratio
			      • Net stable funding ratio

continued on next page

---

[15] During the Global Financial Crisis, regulators learned that many banks around the world had inflated their capital adequacy ratios by loading up on low or zero-risk-weight assets that allowed the banks to meet the regulatory minimum without having sufficient capital to absorb the losses these banks suffered during the crisis.

Table 1 *continued*

	BASEL I	BASEL II	BASEL III
Capital adequacy ratio	• 8% of the risk-weighted assets • Tier 1 capital (equity capital and retained earnings)—equal to or more than 4% • Tier 2 capital—subordinated debt • Total capital: Tier 1 + Tier 2-equal to or more than 8%	• The total capital ratio must be no lower than 8% • Tier 2 capital is limited to 100% of Tier 1 capital	• CET 1: 2% => 4.5% • Minimum capital ratio for commercial banks is 8%, 6% of which must be CET 1 • Capital conservation buffer: 2.5% => 7% • Countercyclical buffer between 0%–2.5% • Leverage ratio: Excess of 3%

CET 1 = common equity tier 1 capital.
Source: Author's compilation.

Impact of Basel III on SMEs. According to the Financial Stability Board (2019), reforms like the Basel III bank regulatory framework will improve long-term financial stability and systemic resilience. However, they might carry short-run costs, and the world is curious to know if SMEs, the main generators of employment and shared prosperity, do incur such costs. The majority of SMEs' external financing comes from banks, so this is the primary mechanism by which reforms would be transmitted to SME growth (FSB 2019).

Under Basel III, it is expected that the impact of the risk-weighted system will become more stringent, which will intensify trends toward less-risky assets. Total capital will still be made up of Tier 1 and Tier 2 components and it will have to account for at least 8% of risk-weighted assets (as in the Basel II Accord). However, the minimum high-quality Tier 1 capital is set at 6% of risk-weighted assets, up from 4% in Basel II, and minimum common equity Tier 1 capital is set at 4.5% of risk-weighted assets, up from Basel II's minimum of just 2%. As a result, the existing reluctance of financial institutions to provide loans to SMEs likely will be exacerbated as banks may prefer to lend to large companies with good credit ratings to ensure a better position to absorb losses.

Capital buffers are a new type of capital requirement introduced by Basel III. The capital-conservation buffer is intended to guarantee that banks set aside money that may be used to absorb losses without causing them to fall below the minimum capital requirement. It is a tool that will help boost sector resilience during times of stress and will provide the mechanism for rebuilding capital outside of those times. Basel III implementation may cause overleveraged and smaller banks to restrict lending access; this is particularly likely to lead to tighter credit access for SMEs, especially for start-up businesses. However, some of Basel III's reforms of the credit-risk calculation method include lowering the risk weight of small-business loans and the loss rate in corporate defaults, which provide countervailing incentives to increase lending to SMEs.

Significant progress has been achieved in the negotiations with the Basel Committee, including the improved treatment of loan exposures to SMEs (up to euro [€]1 million [$1.1 million]) as retail exposure, a significant reduction in the banks' capital requirements for retail loans to SMEs, and in general, a slight reduction of the capital requirements for loans to SMEs. For Basel III, trade finance, particularly in the form of short-term, self-liquidating letters of credit and other similar instruments, has received favorable treatment regarding capital adequacy and liquidity, which is good for SMEs. It will reduce capital requirements for banks engaged in trade finance and thus foster the importation of goods for low-income countries.

Despite these improvements, there were concerns about the adverse impacts of Basel II and Basel III on SME lending. Padgett (2013) argues that initially, higher lender rates and decreased credit availability may force banks to cut down on the amount of lending they extend to SMEs as these potential recipients will have high risk weights that will require greater amounts of capital. Decreased credit availability could impose greater burdens on SMEs that are struggling financially, considering that they were hardest hit despite not being the cause of the 2008–2009 financial crisis. Should these SMEs not be able to secure financing, it may dampen the economy through diminished output and employment, considering the important role of SMEs in fueling economic growth. SMEs will also have to compete with start-up businesses since both the small local businesses and high-potential start-ups will be assigned the same risk; thus, high-potential start-ups may squeeze out small local businesses because of their modest financial returns.

As a precautionary measure, it was imperative to assess any potential unintended consequences of applying a newly created non-risk-based leverage ratio to these instruments that is designed to supplement the capitalization standards through an efficacy check of capital adequacy measurements. Such an assessment reduces incentives for building up high-risk, highly leveraged bank assets that are responsible for any financial dislocation and achieving a safer financial system. Although a consultative document issued by the Financial Stability Board (2019) revealed that no material and persistent negative effects of Basel II and III on SME financing in general due to the enhanced resilience and reduced likelihood and severity of financial crises, there is no one-size-fits-all pattern of implementing the Basel reforms, given differences across jurisdictions. The type of impact and its relative strength may depend on the economic cycle during the reform implementation and may be relatively stronger for jurisdictions affected by an economic crisis. Stakeholder feedback suggests that SME financing trends are largely driven by factors other than financial regulation, such as public policies and macroeconomic conditions, and must be taken carefully into account for better reallocation of credit extended to SMEs.

Efforts toward addressing these concerns were exerted under Basel III to seek a balanced impact on SME lending. As standardized approaches to credit risk assessment may be more appropriate for SME lending than the more complex internal ratings-base applied to large-scale loans, it can provide banks greater ease in lending to SMEs. Greater flexibility in implementing the Basel III rules such as easing the transitional burdens and refusing to impose strict dates for meeting the requirements, according to Padgett (2013), signifies easing some of the negative consequences through careful and gradual implementation of the accord.

Moreover, regulators put in place a number of initiatives to aid and ease the financing of SMEs. Basel II includes three changes aimed at lessening the detrimental effect on financing to SMEs. First, financial institutions may now exchange risk weights for collateral and credit improvements like government guarantees. Financial institutions can substitute the covered portion with the risk weight of the guarantor. Since most credit-guarantee schemes in developing countries were backed by the government, they ended up attracting a 0% risk weight.[16] Second, it reduced the concessional risk weight to 75% from 100% for SME exposures less than euro €1 million. Third, it made an adjustment for banks that used an internal ratings-based approach in the correlation formula for SMEs with total sales or assets below €50 million ($53 million). In December 2017, Basel III reforms introduced a new category—General Corporate SMEs—giving more granularity to unrated risks. SME exposure's risk weight might be reduced by 85%. The risk weight recommendation is based on an examination of SME risk across nations and does not need external assessment. In the Capital Requirements Directives IV, the size factor for SME financing up to €1.5 million ($1.6 million) was adjusted to 0.7619 (i.e., 0.7619*10.5% = 8%) while the size factor for SME financing up to €2.5 million ($2.7 million) was adjusted to 0.85 to lessen the negative impact of Basel III regulations with increased capital requirements (10.5%, including countercyclical buffer) on SME lending. Box 1 looks at the regulatory issues and their consequences.

Box 1: Regulatory Challenges to Small and Medium-Sized Enterprise Lending

Capital and provisions are key factors in extending a loan. Financial institutions keep capital to avoid unprecedented losses associated with loans while provisions are to be implemented for foreseen losses. As per Basel regulations, equity is the most used and desired form of capital. However, it is also the costliest form of capital, so financial institutions may be reluctant to load up on exposures, which leads to higher demand for common equity as capital. Regulations related to the cost of provisioning as well as liquidity and leverage also serve as bottlenecks to small and medium-sized enterprise (SME) financing. The issues and implications are indicated in the table.

Issue	Implication	Consequence
Weak internal ratings-based models	Such models treat large companies and SMEs alike.	SMEs end up getting 100% (or worse) risk weight regardless of years of cash flow and business performance.
Provisioning requirement for a secured loan is cheaper than an unsecured loan	The board and the management are wary about taking assets that can adversely affect their balance sheets.	SMEs that are unable to provide eligible collateral against loan exposures are charged with higher risk premium.
Introduction of liquidity and leverage requirements	The liquidity and leverage framework demands high quality and liquid assets.	SMEs have generally low credit rating and lack flourishing capital market and securitization market so banks refrain from SME exposures.

SMEs = small and medium-sized enterprises.
Source: Author's compilation.

---

16 For example, on an exposure of a $75,000 loan to an SME (attracting a risk weight of 75%) and a capital adequacy ratio of 8%, the capital requirement would be as follows: Unguaranteed Loan: $75,000 * 75% * 8% = $4,500 guaranteed loan with 90% coverage: 90% * $75,000 * 0% * 8% + 10% * $75,000 * 75% * 8% = $450 (90% reduction in capital).

Reflecting the new category in Basel III, the Republic of Korea's financial supervisory authority expanded the scope of SME recognition to Korean won (W) 70 billion in sales and improved related standards. This meant that about 9,000 corporates could be classified as SMEs based on the revised regulation (Box 2). In addition, incentives were given to a bank's SME loan handling by revising the detailed rules for banking supervision so that, when banks calculate the BIS ratio using its internal credit rating model, a lower risk weight is applied for SME loans than that for general companies.

Box 2: New Classification of Small and Medium-Sized Enterprises by the Financial Services Commission under Basel III

For Basel III, the Financial Services Commission in the Republic of Korea implemented a policy to streamline banks' capital regulations on small and medium-sized enterprise (SME) lending. Key features are highlighted in the table.

	Current	Revision
Expanding the scope of SMEs	SMEs with total sales of less than W60 billion	SMEs with total sales of less than W70 billion
Expanding the criteria for SMEs	Only SMEs can be recognized by total sales	SMEs can be recognized by total sales or total assets
Eliminating disadvantages for new companies	Regarded as a general enterprise due to lack of corporate information	Regarded as an SME
Effect	Due to these new provisions, about 9,000 corporate borrowers were classified as SMEs whose risk weight is down to 75% from 100%. As a result, the capital burden of lenders dealing with SME loans has been reduced, improving lending capacity for SMEs. Furthermore, the interest burden on SME borrowers has been eased.	

SMEs = small and medium-sized enterprises, W = Korean won.
Source: Author's compilation.

Small and Medium-Sized Enterprise Public Lending: The Case of the Republic of Korea

Inadequate financing due to a lack of information remains a major obstacle for SMEs to grow and improve performance. The following case study illustrates measures implemented in the Republic of Korea to improve access to credit through a dedicated SME lending bank—the IBK. The Republic of Korea case also demonstrates that public support—through various ministries and public corporations—is instrumental in developing SME finance and credit infrastructure.

Small and Medium-Sized Enterprise Support Systems in the Republic of Korea

In the Republic of Korea, SMEs have been receiving strong support from the government for the past 50 years, regardless of changes in government or economic policy. At the beginning of the implementation of the economic development policy, in the 1970s, the Korean government focused on fostering SMEs and developing heavy and chemical industries. Economic power was thus concentrated in big conglomerates which made the government drive its support to foster SMEs as a countermeasure to pursue balanced and inclusive economic growth. The government has since passed laws enhancing both governmental and private support to SMEs.

Experience in many countries suggests that sustainable growth is possible when SME-based economic growth, job creation, and innovative technology development and their connected network become the basis of the overall economy. In this regard, public policy in the Republic of Korea has emphasized the importance of improving the competitiveness of SMEs for achieving the competitiveness of large enterprises. The Korean government for this reason established a comprehensive support system for SMEs.

It is the responsibility of the Ministry of SMEs and Startups to create and conduct national policies that encourage entrepreneurship, SMEs, and firm growth. Apart from the IBK for SME financing, Figure 1 shows nine affiliated institutions that support SMEs.

Figure 1: Small and Medium-Sized Enterprise Support Systems in the Republic of Korea

SMEs = small and medium-sized enterprises.
Source: The Ministry of SMEs and Startups.

The Industrial Bank of Korea

History

As can be seen in Figure 2, IBK was founded in 1961 as a public bank under the Industrial Bank of Korea Act to offer financial services to SMEs with restricted access to market resources.[17] The bank has grown significantly, with its expansion accelerating in the 1980s as the government's industrial policy shifted from export-oriented big businesses to technology-intensive SMEs. Since 1981, IBK has given policy loans to SMEs that manufacture and sell various intermediate goods—such as diverse parts, industrial materials, and tools—to large firms.

In 1989, IBK began offering policy loans to small businesses with high growth potential and fewer than 50 staff. Because these small businesses usually had trouble acquiring loans from traditional banks, which require collateral, IBK gave policy loans without collateral. Policy loans from IBK dramatically increased from $1.6 billion in 1980 to $9.4 billion in 1990 as a result.

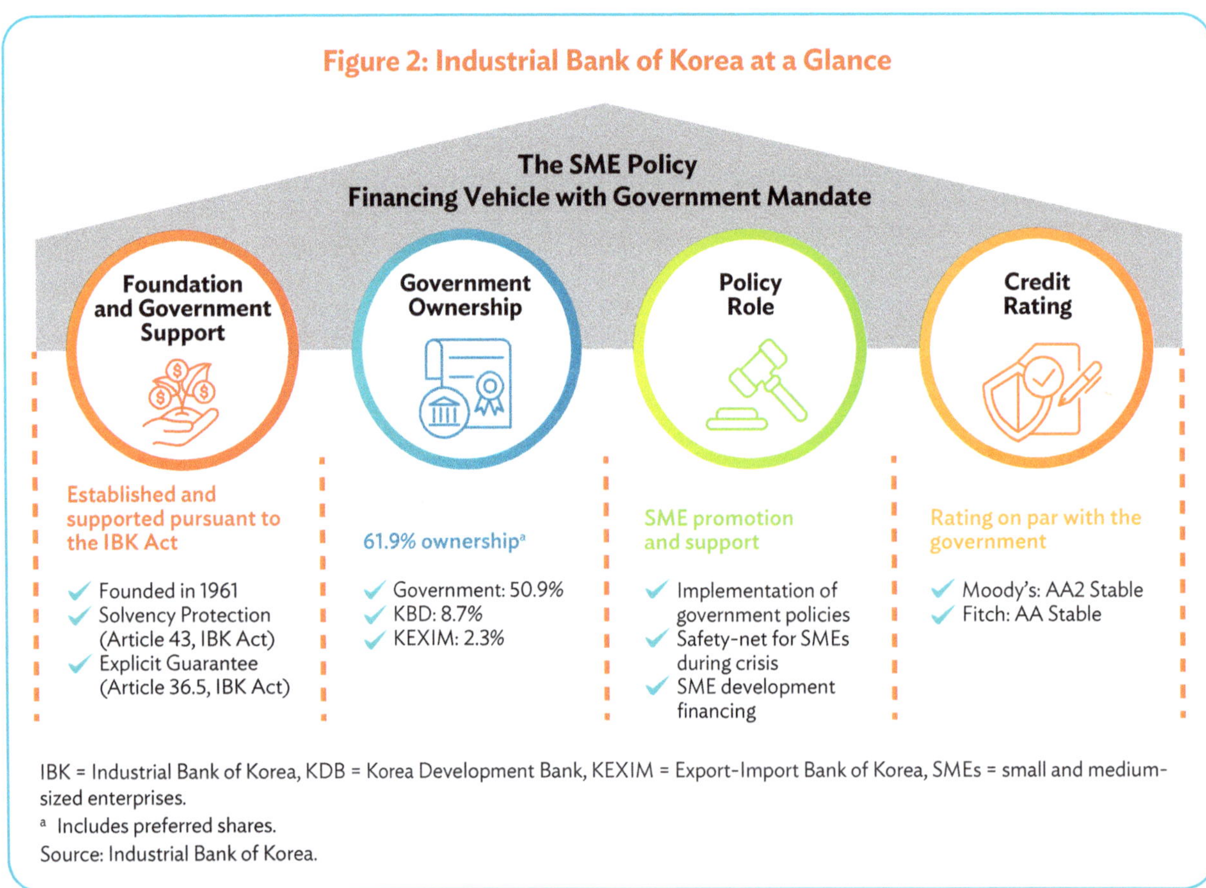

IBK = Industrial Bank of Korea, KDB = Korea Development Bank, KEXIM = Export-Import Bank of Korea, SMEs = small and medium-sized enterprises.
a Includes preferred shares.
Source: Industrial Bank of Korea.

---

17   A significant portion of this section is based on internal IBK documents and reports from the Korea Development Institute.

Figure 3 shows the development of the Industrial Bank of Korea. Total loans (including policy loans) from IBK rose dramatically from W2.6 billion ($1.9 million) in 1961 to W273 trillion ($208 billion) in 2022.

In addition to IBK's SME-specified public bank, the bank served as an agency for providing credit guarantees for SME loans. Prior to the establishment of the Korea Credit Guarantee Fund (KODIT), IBK was the only SME-specialized institution which offers not only loans, but credit guarantees. In March 1967, IBK established the Credit Guarantee Fund with contributions from government and banks and initially served as the implementing agency and manager of the guarantee fund.[18] Since then, however, the scale of guarantee services has increased, as has the need for effective asset management of the fund and expertise in guarantee services. Moreover, as conflicts of interest for the lender (IBK) to provide guarantees for its own loans emerged, the Korean government enacted a new Credit Guarantee Fund Law in December 1974 and established KODIT separately from the IBK.

Meanwhile, IBK has tried to expand credit lending with a focus on creditworthiness and business feasibility to support SMEs. In December 1990, the bank introduced the "credit loan limit system" for the first time among domestic financial institutions and established institutional means for expanding credit services for SMEs. And since 1991, IBK has made it possible to lend within certain limits without the need for physical collateral or a joint guarantor, which has greatly contributed to reducing financial costs and simplifying lending procedures. The IBK, in particular, converted to a credit lending system that would relieve SMEs of financial pressures by introducing credit-value-based loan procedures.

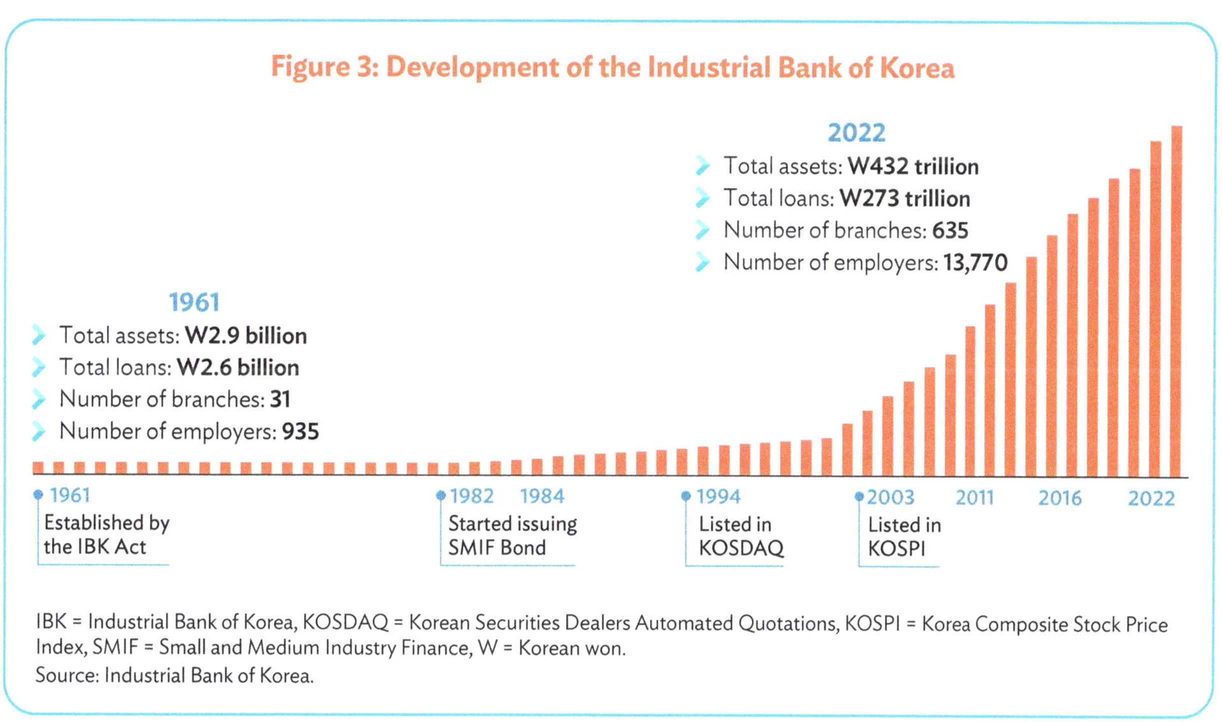

IBK = Industrial Bank of Korea, KOSDAQ = Korean Securities Dealers Automated Quotations, KOSPI = Korea Composite Stock Price Index, SMIF = Small and Medium Industry Finance, W = Korean won.
Source: Industrial Bank of Korea.

---

[18] Based on Article 15 of the SME Banking Law Enforcement Ordinance (established in 1961), when making loans to SMEs, IBK collected and accumulated a portion of credit guarantee costs. This made it possible to supplement collateral for credit loans, and coverage by reserves was expanded up to 10 times reserves.

And in 1995, IBK was the first domestic financial institution to develop a credit rating evaluation model for SMEs. Its Credit Scoring System became a turning point in the provision of unsecured loans to SMEs without collateral and built a credit society in the Korean financial system.

On the funding side, since 1982, IBK has increased its funding sources by issuing Small and Medium Industry Finance (SMIF) bonds to meet IBK's increasing loan portfolio, as well as deposits. In addition to direct lending services to SMEs, IBK in 1990 started an investment banking business to support financing for SMEs by utilizing funding tools from the capital markets. This includes issuing securities, stock, and debenture underwriting, and securities purchases and sales.

Special Mandates of the Industrial Bank of Korea

As noted, the IBK Act facilitates Industrial Bank of Korea's outreach to SMEs. SMEs should get at least 70% of their overall loan portfolio, as seen in Table 2, and the government provides it funds to cover deficits incurred and guarantees interest and principal payments of IBK's SMIF bonds. Furthermore, IBK is subject to easier liquidity ratios, at 70%, exemption from the loan-to-deposit ratio of 100%, and an issuance limit of SMIF bonds that is up to 20 times paid in capital and reserves (Figure 4).

Table 2: Key Features of the Industrial Bank of Korea Act

Purpose	To promote the independent economic activities of small and medium-sized enterprises (SMEs) and enhance SMEs' economic position in the national economy	Article 1
Governance	President of the Republic of Korea appoints the president and Chief Executive Officer (CEO) of Industrial Bank of Korea (IBK)	Article 26
Business plan	Government approves IBK's annual business plan	Article 35
SME lending	At least 70% of total loan portfolio for SMEs	Enforcement Decree 31
SME research	Conduct research and business consultation for SMEs	Article 33.3
Solvency protection	Government shall provide funds to cover IBK's deficit	Article 43
Explicit IBK bonds	Government may provide guarantee on the payment of interest and principal of IBK's bonds, subject to the approval from the National Assembly	Article 36.5

IBK = Industrial Bank of Korea, SMEs = small and medium-sized enterprises.
Source: Author's compilation.

Loan portfolio and clients

Figure 5 compares IBK's clients to the Republic of Korea's major commercial banks, as well as loan composition by loan size, number of staff, and industry. SMEs accounted for 78.9% of IBK's loans in the first quarter of 2018, accounting for 22.6% of the nation's SME market. In its SME loans, 78.6% were less than $0.5 million, 89.5% went to businesses with 10 or fewer personnel, and 60.0% of the loans went to the manufacturing sector.

Figure 4: Key Provisions for the Industrial Bank of Korea

SME Loan Ratio

> Mandated to provide more than 70% of total funding to SMEs in loan

Liquidity Ratio

> Eased liquidity ratios to 70%

Loan-to-Deposit Ratio

> Exempted from loan-to-deposit ratio requirements of 100%

SMIF Bond

> Issuance limit up to 20 times the paid-in-capital and reserves whereas, other commercial banks can only issue 3 times the paid-in-capital
> Counted as SME lending when foreign banks in Republic of Korea need to comply with SME lending requirement (35%)
> Zero risk rating when calculating BIS ratio (commercial bank notes 20%)

BIS = Bank for International Settlements, SMEs = small and medium-sized enterprises, SMIF = small and medium industry finance.
Source: Industrial Bank of Korea. 2016. *New Future in Finance for SMEs*. Seoul.

Figure 5: Breakdown of Industrial Bank of Korea Small and Medium-Sized Enterprise Loan Portfolio
(%)

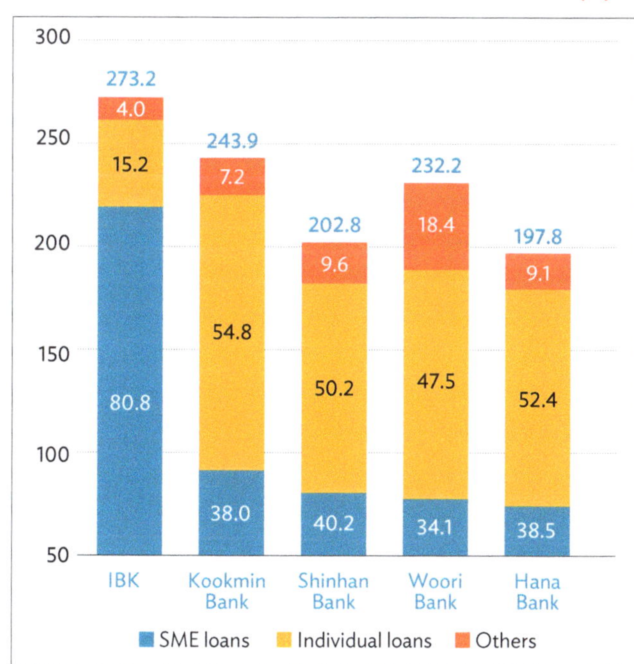

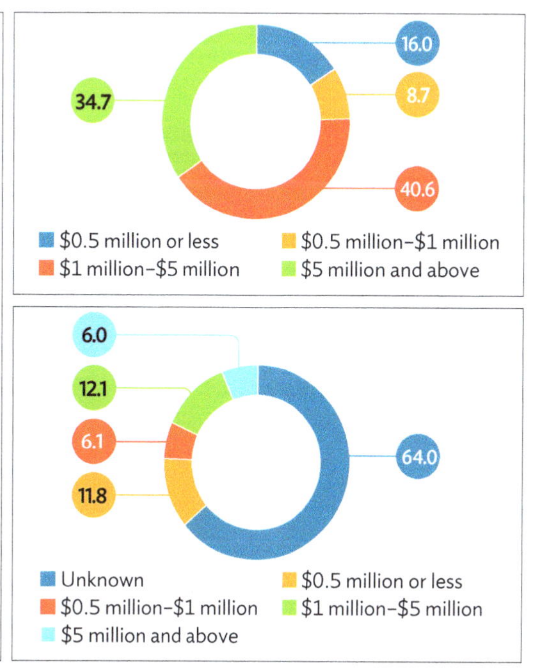

IBK = Industrial Bank of Korea, SME = small and medium-sized enterprise, .
Source: IBK Fact Book as of the end of 2022 (Other Korean Banks' loan breakdown is as of the first quarter of 2018).

As of the first half of 2022 (Table 3), unsecured loans comprised 16.6% of the SME loan portfolio.

Table 3: Unsecured Loans for Small and Medium-Sized Enterprises by the Industrial Bank of Korea

	2019		2020		2021		2022	
	Amount (W trillion)	Ratio (%)	Amount (W trillion)	Ratio (%)	Amount (W trillion)	Ratio (%)	Amount (W trillion)	Ratio (%)
SME Loan	**166.5**	**100**	**186.8**	**100**	**203.9**	**100**	**220.7**	**100**
Collateral	91.5	54.9	116.9	62.6	131.5	64.5	146.3	66.3
Guaranteed	27.7	16.7	36.0	19.3	37.5	18.4	37.6	17.1
Unsecured	47.3	28.4	33.9	18.1	34.8	17.1	36.7	16.6

SMEs = small and medium-sized enterprises, W = Korean won.
Source: IBK IR Factbook (Loans and Deposit). https://global.ibk.co.kr/en/investor/FactBook (accessed 4/12/2022)

Since IBK's privatization in 1994, its financial performance has been positive and competitive with other commercial banks despite SME loans constituting a high percentage of its total loan portfolio.[19] IBK's banking business is comparable to traditional banking institutions in the Republic of Korea in terms of service areas, business performance, and compliance with banking regulations.

Funding structure

Currently, IBK's funding consists of deposits and SMIF bonds. SMIF bonds procured were 54.5% of total funding (depositary) in 2022 (Table 4). In addition, 54% of IBK's SMIF bonds (29.4% of the total) were sold through branch networks and the remaining 46% through the capital market. Branch networks account for a high share because, as the SMIF bonds are not subject to deposit insurance fees, these can give customers a higher interest rate than the general deposit rate provided by other banks.

Table 4: Industrial Bank of Korea Bonds Out of Total Depositary

	2019		2020		2021		2022	
	Amount (W trillion)	Ratio (%)	Amount (W trillion)	Ratio (%)	Amount (W trillion)	Ratio (%)	Amount (W trillion)	Ratio (%)
Total Depository	214.2	100	239.1	100	265.2	100	280.1	100
IBK Bonds	**115.4**	**53.9**	**122.1**	**51.1**	**132.7**	**50.0**	**152.7**	**54.5**
Branch	65.1	56.4	59.7	48.9	64.2	48.4	82.4	54.0
Market	50.3	43.6	62.4	51.1	68.5	51.6	70.3	46.0

IBK = Industrial Bank of Korea, W = Korean won.
Source: Industrial Bank of Korea. Annual reports. https://global.ibk.co.kr/en/investor/AnnualReport.

---

[19] Until 1994, the Korean government held IBK's entire issued share capital. Since 1994, the government's ownership has gradually decreased through public offerings of new shares and an increase in employee stock ownership. As of 31 December 2022, the government's share is at 59.5%, from 63.7% last 1 May 2021. https://global.ibk.co.kr/en/investor/ChangeinShareRatioofGovernment.

Major Roles of the Industrial Bank of Korea

Fostering economic growth through SME development. IBK has played an essential and pioneering role in the industrialization and economic development of the Republic of Korea through its financial support for the growth of SMEs as seen in Figure 6.

It is the only policy bank responsible for directly funding SMEs and it has contributed to the number of SMEs, the number of employees, the proportion of SMEs in GDP, and others. As such, IBK's SME clients have grown steadily, reaching more than 2.1 million, accounting for 26.7% of SMEs in the Republic of Korea as of 2020 (Figure 6).

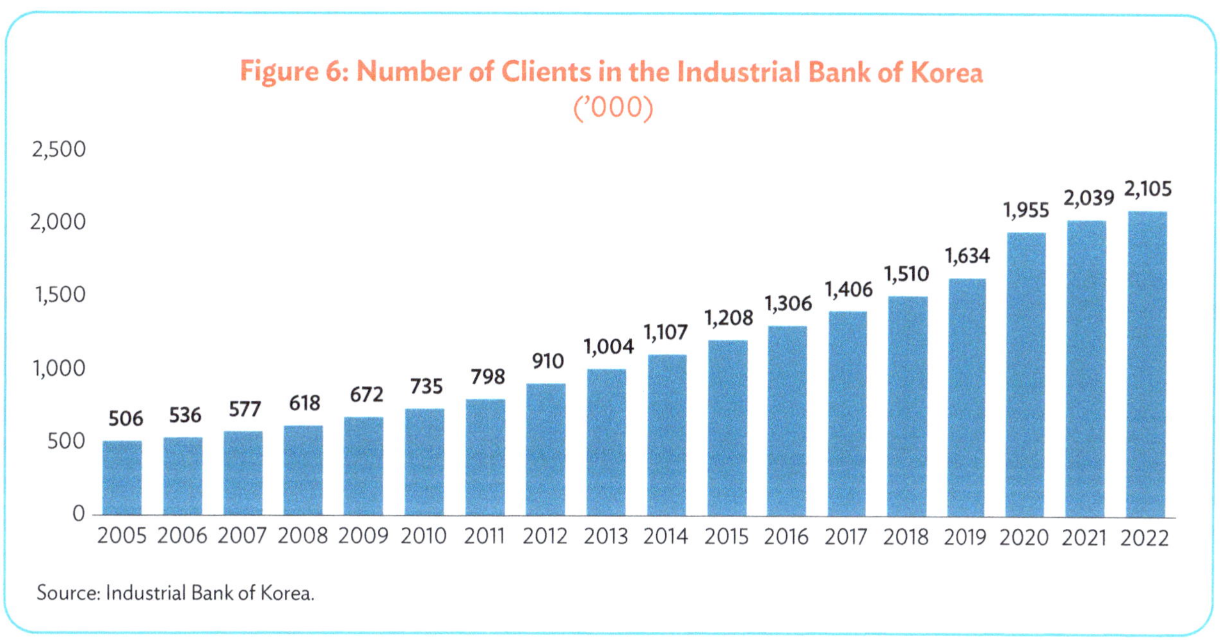

Figure 6: Number of Clients in the Industrial Bank of Korea
('000)

Source: Industrial Bank of Korea.

Overcoming market failure caused by information asymmetry. IBK is critical for overcoming market failure, which is primarily caused by a shortage of private voluntary funding for high-risk SMEs. IBK systematically embodies and systemizes information on SMEs that have accumulated over a long period of time. This enables the institution to develop specialized financial products for SMEs, ultimately narrowing the gap in financing of these smaller firms left by commercial banks or other financial intermediaries. IBK is equipped with the "Advanced Internal Ratings-Based Approach" under Basel II, the financial regulation authority approved. Furthermore, the institution maintains a stable capital structure and profitable business. And to reiterate, IBK provides a relatively higher rate of unsecured loans to SMEs than other commercial banks—about 17%, almost double of other domestic banks such as Kookmin Bank and Hana Bank (Table 5).

Table 5: Unsecured Small and Medium-Sized Enterprise Loans among Major Korean Banks

	2018		2019		2020		2021		2022	
	Amount (W trillion)	Ratio (%)	Amount (W trillion)	Ratio (%)	Amount (W trillion)	Ratio (%)	Amount (W trillion)	Ratio (%)	Amount (W trillion)	Ratio (%)
IBK	34.0	17.9	33.2	17.2	33.9	16.8	34.8	17.1	36.7	16.6
Kookmin	17.0	8.9	17.2	8.9	19.2	9.5				
Shinhan	23.7	12.4	22.6	11.7	23.3	11.6				
Woori	30.1	15.8	32.4	16.8	34.6	17.2	No data			
Hana	15.5	8.1	16.3	8.4	16.7	8.3				
Others	70.1	36.8	71.7	37.1	74	36.7				
Total	190.4	100	193.4	100	201.7	100	203.6	100	221.1	100

IBK = Industrial Bank of Korea, W = Korean won.
Source: Korea Federation of Banks and Industrial Bank of Korea.

A key role to support SMEs during the COVID-19 pandemic. During the COVID-19 pandemic, IBK provided the largest amount of SME financing. This position at the forefront of support for SMEs during economic turmoil is made clear in Table 6, with active increases in SME loans during the liquidity issues that tend to come with financial crisis. IBK has provided a safety net for SMEs through liquidity injection in economic turmoil.

Table 6: Small and Medium-Sized Enterprise Financing during COVID-19

	March 2020	April 2020	
	Amount (W trillion)	Amount (W trillion)	Increase (%)
Industrial Bank of Korea	168.7	181.6	7.6
Kookmin Bank	107.8	114.3	6.1
Shinhan Bank	94.4	100.2	6.1
Woori Bank	85.2	90.5	6.2
Hana Bank	87.9	92.2	5.0
Total	544.0	578.8	6.4

COVID-19 = coronavirus disease, W = Korean won.
Source: Financial Supervisory Committee.

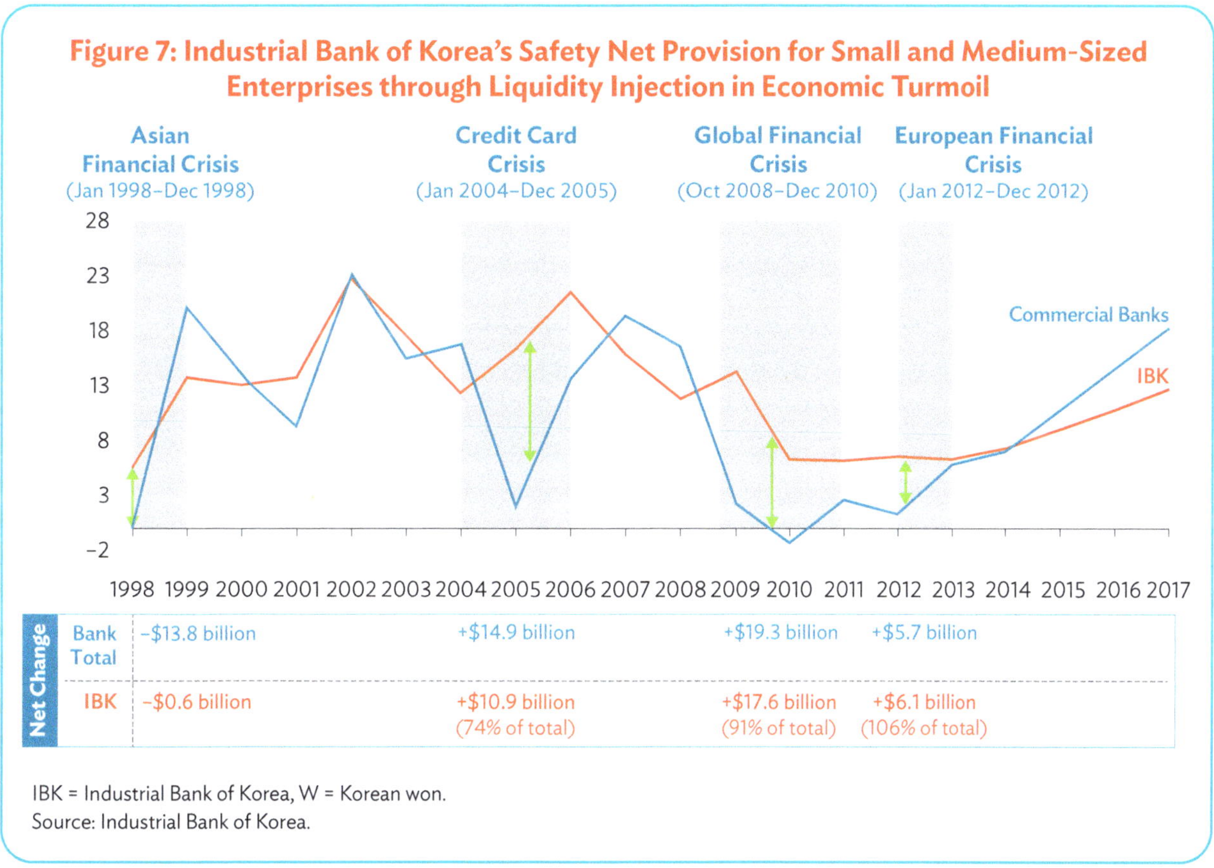

Figure 7: Industrial Bank of Korea's Safety Net Provision for Small and Medium-Sized Enterprises through Liquidity Injection in Economic Turmoil

Net Change					
Bank Total	–$13.8 billion	+$14.9 billion		+$19.3 billion	+$5.7 billion
IBK	–$0.6 billion	+$10.9 billion (74% of total)		+$17.6 billion (91% of total)	+$6.1 billion (106% of total)

IBK = Industrial Bank of Korea, W = Korean won.
Source: Industrial Bank of Korea.

Activation of private sector participation. Even though its business is mostly limited to SMEs, IBK has generated favorable earnings and has encouraged the participation of commercial banks in the SME financing market.[20] As noted earlier, while SMEs are generally considered risky, IBK has successfully maintained sound asset quality.[21] Generally, lending to SMEs is sensitive to the business cycle, and a recession often results in impaired loans. Nevertheless, through its effective utilization of the abundant bank data of MSMEs and its credit analysis and measurement capacities, IBK has demonstrated effective and superior screening and monitoring for SME lending. Indeed, it remains the top expert in SME finance, pioneering new markets, and attracting private sector financing to SMEs.

IBK provides funding in the four different business stages of SMEs: start-up, technical development, commercialization, and globalization. Its transaction coverage varies from funding for production to funding for collection of accounts receivable. It also offers advisory services to SMEs at all stages of their development.

In the first stage, IBK is particularly active in finding and nurturing SMEs with fewer than five employees. At the second stage, technology development, IBK provides research and development funding and commercialization preparations, such as funding for prototype development. To do this, the institution

20 Total Net Income (Cumulative, W in billion): 2018: 1,511.0, 2019: 1,392.9, 2020: 1,263.2, 2021: 2,024.1, 2022: 2,454.8; IBK Fact Book 2022, Financial Highlights (accessed 5 May 2023).
21 NPL Ratio from 2019–2021: 2018: 1.36%, 2019: 1.30%, 2020: 1.17%, 2021:0.93%, 2022: 0.82%; IBK Fact Book 2022, Source: IBK Fact Book 2022 (accessed 5 May 2023).

operates a separate division to evaluate the technology of SMEs, providing long-term funding of over 7 years. At the third stage—commercialization—IBK provides working capital loans, facilities loans, sales facilities loans, and many other financial products to SMEs. At the fourth stage, globalization, IBK provides resources to SMEs through funds from international organizations, equity investment, and initial public offerings, overseas consulting, and more.

Diverse financing products and services. Many SMEs are exposed to liquidity problems due to many factors such as increasing raw material prices and delays in the delivery of goods. Payment delays for items delivered are a particular issue. IBK created network loans to help with cash flow, which are provided based on purchase orders provided by purchasers and reimbursed to IBK bank (Figure 8).

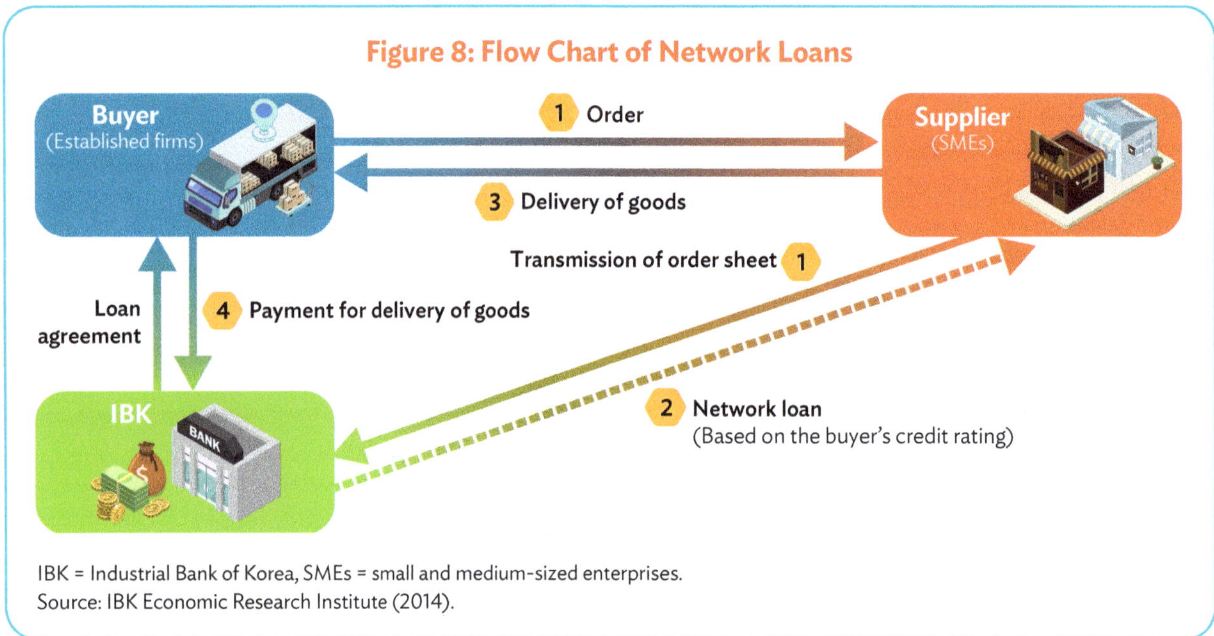

IBK = Industrial Bank of Korea, SMEs = small and medium-sized enterprises.
Source: IBK Economic Research Institute (2014).

First, IBK undertakes network loan business contracts with established buyers (or firms). These established buyers are audited by an external agency if the asset exceeds $12 million. The buyers must also hold a BBB or higher credit rating to sign this business agreement. For this buyer's credit-based loan scheme, buyers need to place an order with the supplier and send the order sheet to IBK. IBK then provides the supplier with a network loan, subject to the terms of the business contract. Network loans are computed based on the buyer's strong credit rating, in which interest is relatively cheaper than regular credit. Cross-subsidization through a credit guarantee scheme (with KODIT, for example) can be applied in cases where the buyer's credit rating is not enough. In this case, the credit risk is simply shared between IBK and a credit guarantee scheme. The network loan is an important tool to support SMEs as they are engaged in value chain businesses with large companies which has a BBB or better credit rating. So, the SMEs in the value chain would benefit from this network loan with higher ratings of reputable buyers. Also, through this network loans, many SMEs have been able to favorably access credit services by IBK and build up their financial records which help them access more credit services.

In addition, IBK provides complete consulting services in all sectors of business. SMEs face non financial barriers related to management capabilities, and IBK has promoted strengthening of these and technological development in SMEs.

In the early 1960s, Korean SMEs were underdeveloped. Their management style was outdated, their facilities were exhausted, and their capital stock was depleted. It was very difficult to adapt to new environments with financial assistance alone. Better results clearly would not be achieved without improving these factors, motivating IBK to strengthen its corporate guidance project.

In 1962, the IBK established the Corporate Guidance Department in 1962 and created the SME Consultation Center, which offered financial, management, accounting, and taxes consultation and education. Initially, consulting work undertook corporate management, but gradually expanded to other relevant areas, such as pilot training programs, on-site analytics, one-on-one consulting, and the establishment and operation of export centers. Over the years, the bank's guidance has become more diverse and efficient.

In the 1980s, the bank held SME Chief Executive Officer (CEO) seminars to reflect the current concerns of SMEs. It aimed to strengthen communication and cooperation between banks and SMEs and collect customer recommendations to diversify financial products and improve quality of banking services. The bank established a corporate information center in May 1989 to improve the operation of its existing SME service center. The center promptly delivers diverse business information linked to corporate management for SMEs that are experiencing trouble accessing information. IBK also provides consultation on overseas investment.

In addition, in 1990, IBK opened its permanent exhibition hall at the head office to promote SME products. Banks also complemented the marketing activities of SMEs by mediating trade and providing consultation on the export markets of local SMEs. In January 1996, in particular, IBK started offering consultation services for mergers and acquisitions, which helps SMEs strengthen competitiveness and diversify business areas. Finally, in 2015, IBK launched the "SMEs Hope Consulting Project," which provided SMEs with consulting services on business management, taxation, and laws. IBK delivers roughly 1,000 free consulting services each year through these programs.

Risk management system. The bank also developed a risk management system in cooperation with other institutions such as credit rating agencies (Figure 9). It analyzes credit risks to maintain excellent asset quality management and continuously monitors any changes in the borrowers' credit risk. IBK's real time-based automatic adequacy assessment enables it to identify at-risk enterprises quickly and execute preemptive restructuring to assist in the rehabilitation of businesses with high credit risk.

IBK has made a major contribution to SME lending despite the risks involved. its capital adequacy ratios have continuously risen and continue to be above Basel II regulatory standards (Figure 10).

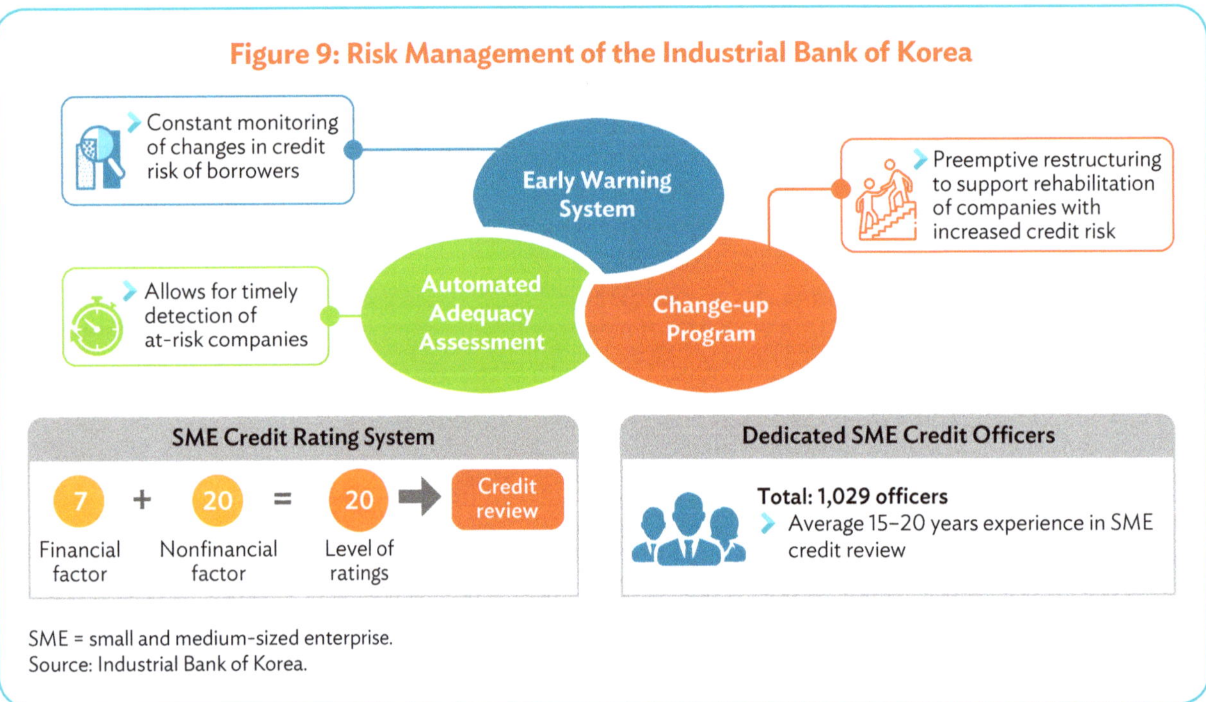

Figure 9: Risk Management of the Industrial Bank of Korea

SME = small and medium-sized enterprise.
Source: Industrial Bank of Korea.

Figure 10: Capital Adequacy of the Industrial Bank of Korea

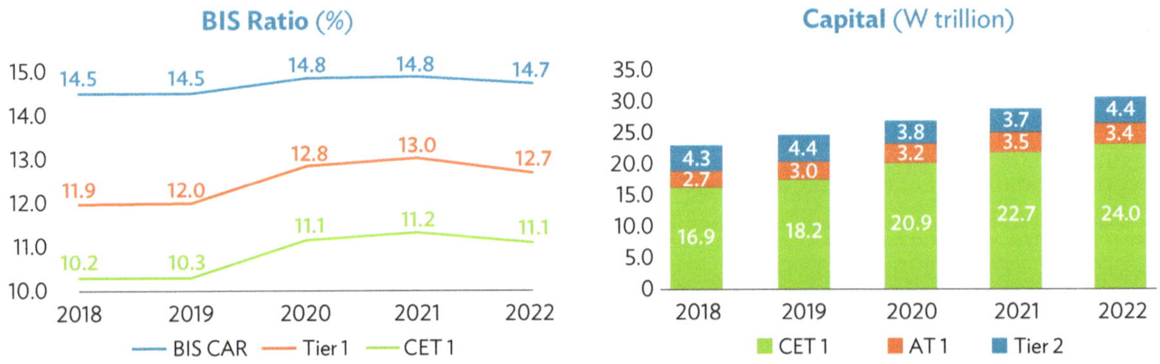

	2018	2019	2020	2021	2022
Equity Capital	23.9	25.5	27.8	29.6	31.8
Tier 1 Capital (A)	19.6	21.1	24.1	26.1	27.4
Common Equity Tier 1 Capital	16.9	18.2	20.9	22.7	24.0
Additional Tier 1 Capital	2.7	3.0	3.2	3.5	3.4
Tier 2 Capital (B)	4.3	4.4	3.8	3.5	4.4
Risk-Weighted Assets	165.0	176.3	187.8	200.8	216.6
BIS Capital Adequacy Ratio	14.50%	14.47%	14.82%	14.85%	14.68%
Tier 1 Ratio	11.90%	11.97%	12.82%	13.01%	12.67%
Common Equity Tier 1 Ratio	10.24%	10.30%	11.13%	11.29%	11.08%
Tier 2 Ratio	2.60%	2.50%	2.01%	1.83%	2.01%

AT 1= additional tier 1 capital, BIS = Bank for International Settlements, CET 1 = common equity tier 1 capital, W = Korean won.
Source: Industrial Bank of Korea.

The three stages of IBK's risk management process are pre-lending assessment, interim review, and aftercare (Figure 11).

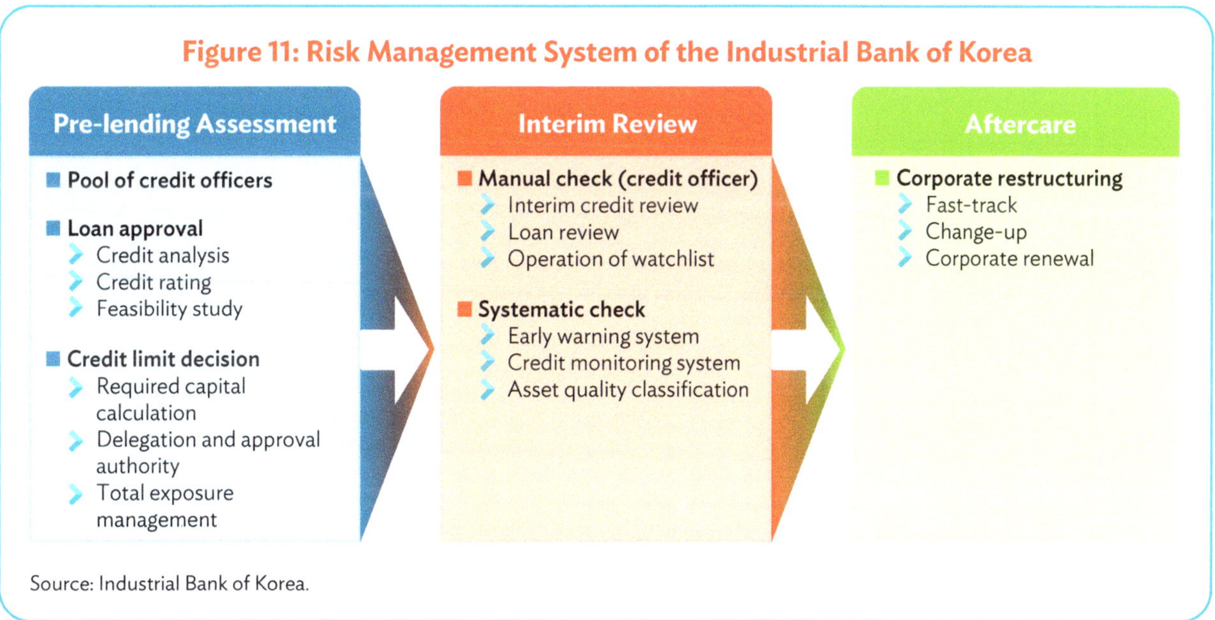

Figure 11: Risk Management System of the Industrial Bank of Korea

Source: Industrial Bank of Korea.

The decision-making phase before the loan is known as pre-lending assessment. Table 7 illustrates the main system of this process. After the loan has been disbursed, the interim review stage begins. Manual checks done directly by professional credit officers and systematic checks filtered by various systems are the two primary categories (Table 8). The final stage of risk management is aftercare. During the interim review process, it predominantly affects SME borrowers who might be on the brink of bankruptcy.

Table 7: Highlights of the Pre-Lending Assessment of the Industrial Bank of Korea

Pre-Lending Assessment		Highlights	Frequency
Loan approval	Credit analysis	• Conduct time series analysis on the applicant's past, present, and future financial status and other operational information	Annually
	Credit rating	• Investigate the applicant's overall information such as assess repayment capacity and commitment and then classify into 19 credit ratings (AAA+ ~ D) to use it for loan approval	Annually
	Feasibility study	• Study feasibility of new business to make loan decision	Annually
Credit limit decision	Required capital calculation	• Consider applying company's revenue, repayment capacity, and other information to calculate appropriate level of required capital	Before origination
	Delegation of approval authority	• Consider the company's credit rating, collateral, and risk associated with the loan product	Before origination
	Total exposure	• Set up and control total credit limit for large borrowers ($30 million or over for corporate loan customers)	Internal policy

Source: Industrial Bank of Korea.

Table 8: Highlights of the Interim Review of the Industrial Bank of Korea

		Highlights	Frequency
Manual check	Interim credit examination	• Check possible changes in credit risk, aside from regular credit analysis, to prevent insolvency and strength asset management	Annually
	Loan review	• Re-examine payment capacity, compliance of relevant regulations and/or policies at the time of origination, appropriateness of loan approval, and others.	As needed
	Watchlist system	• Review credit risk and take appropriate measures for companies showing abnormal signals	As needed
Systematic check	Early warning system	• Make system check on possible changes in corporate credit risk and classify into five categories (blue, green, yellow, amber, red)	Daily
	Credit monitoring system	• Monitor appropriateness of credit rating and make necessary adjustment following the monitoring	As needed
	Asset quality classification	• Classify into five categories (normal, precautionary, substandard, doubtful, and estimated loss) depending on repayment capacity, length of delinquency, default status, and others, and use it for loan loss provisioning	Monthly

Source: Industrial Bank of Korea.

IBK uses an automated early warning system to check SMEs' credit risk on a daily basis. The credit monitoring system checks the validity of the current credit rating as needed and, if any issues affect it, adjusts its computation based on the new issues. Meanwhile, an early monitoring system was developed to monitor any changes in credit risk raised by market, financial, and business conditions—managed and controlled by specialized credit officers to assess asset quality classification monthly. The superiority of IBK in interim review is a judgment of the timing of SME insolvency. In contrast to Korean commercial banks, which used the same credit rating models both for large firms and SMEs, IBK developed and used a system specific to SMEs. In 1995, IBK developed Korea's first SME credit rating model, based on IBK's extensive database of SMEs and on the empirical knowledge of IBK's credit analysts and officers.

As IBK has established a loan review system specialized for SMEs in the interim review stage, the criteria for judging the possibility of rehabilitation begin to differ from those of other banks, with the advantage of being able to more accurately determine whether SMEs are insolvent. While other private banks determine whether SMEs are insolvent according to the overall business conditions and financial market conditions, IBK uses a loan review system specialized for SMEs, so that the timing and support for SMEs recoverable through financial support can be differentiated.

Overall, the risk management process contributes to IBK's low delinquency rate, at 0.34%–0.52% point lower than the industry average following the global financial crisis of 2008. However, rates do not differ significantly between IBK and the industry average in recent years. Nevertheless, IBK's special financial products, such as win-win collaboration loans, still record a delinquency rate 0.10% point lower than those of IBK as of 2021 (Table 9).

Table 9: Delinquency Ratio in Small and Medium-Sized Enterprise Loans
(%)

	2015	2016	2017	2018	2019	2020	2021	2022
Industry average (A)	1.15	1.50	0.48	0.49	0.44		No data	
Industrial Bank of Korea (B)	0.81	0.98	0.42	0.51	0.51	0.39	0.28	0.34
Win-win collaboration loan[a] (C)	No data	0.29	0.21	0.33	0.35	0.20	0.10	0.25
B-A		−0.34	−0.52	−0.06	0.02	0.07		No data
C-B		No data	−0.69	−0.21	−0.18	−0.16	−0.19	−0.18	−0.09

SMEs = small and medium-sized enterprises.

[a] The impact of the 2008 global financial crisis has created a social consensus on shared growth. Thus, a win-win collaboration loan was developed during 2019 to provide loans to the partner SMEs of large enterprises by utilizing the financial resources deposited by large enterprises in IBK. In other words, large enterprises deposit the surplus cash without receiving interest from IBK, and then IBK uses these funds by providing low-interest loans to the partner SMEs. Meanwhile, large enterprises may receive tax credit or incentives when bidding for government products according to their funding performance.

Sources: IADB (2015) and Industrial Bank of Korea (internal data).

Table 10: Highlights of Corporate Restructuring of the Industrial Bank of Korea

Test	Result	Action
Corporate Credit Risk Assessment	Normally operable	**Fast-Track program**
	Possible to show trouble signals later	• Maintain existing loans to enable normal business operation • Provide liquidity for temporary cash-strapped companies * Recommend management improvement, sign a special agreement on self-help plan, if needed
	Currently with trouble signals, but with possibility of normalization	**Work-out (Change-up)** • Loan rescheduling, rate cuts, new liquidity support, debt-to-equity swap, and others.
	Currently with trouble signals, without possibility of normalization	**Corporate renewal or collection** • Court receivership • Collection through legal process

Source: Industrial Bank of Korea.

Current corporate rehabilitation support programs. IBK activates customized rehabilitation support programs for SMEs whose financial condition is at risk. Three programs—Change-up, Fast-Track, and Pre-FTP (Fast-Track Program)—are applied dependent upon the corporate situation (Table 10).[22] This is determined considering the SME's insolvency progress, the complexity of the creditor structure, and the intensity of restructuring. IBK preemptively supports the structural adjustment of such marginal SMEs. A representative example is the pre-FTP procedure. It supports corporate recovery programs that provide interest rate reductions, principal repayment postponements, and additional operating fund provisions toward selected borrowers whose liquidity has temporarily deteriorated due to exterior problems and who can normalize soon.

---

[22] Change-up is a procedure for promoting business normalization through debt adjustment support and voluntary self-reliance plans for companies (both large enterprise and SMEs) that have been selected for restructuring in compliance with the regulations of the financial supervisory authority and are eligible for business normalization. In Fast-Track, banks holding loans jointly support liquidity for SMEs experiencing temporary liquidity shortages. In contrast, pre-FTP is a new procedure to support liquidity solely by IBK for SMEs experiencing temporary liquidity shortages since September 2015.

On the other hand, chronic impaired loans are immediately transferred to IBK headquarters and disposed of quickly. Tables 11 and 12 show that IBK's corporate rehabilitation support program is divided into new and existing programs according to three types of rehabilitation program. The number of SMEs and executed amount are listed.

Table 11: Corporate Rehabilitation Support Programs

	2017		2018		2019		2020		2021		2022	
	No. of SMEs	Amount (W billion)	No. of SMEs	Amount (W billion)	No. of SMEs	Amount (W billion)	No. of SMEs	Amount (W billion)	No. of SMEs	Amount (W billion)	No. of SMEs	Amount (W billion)
Change-Up	269	1,336.7	200	830.6	184	807.2	110	302.9	67	281.8	179	287.7
Fast-Track	87	297.6	104	420.9	170	789.8	118	659.0	90	500.5	63	326.8
Pre-FTP	82	386.2	57	250.5	53	307.2	91	474.4	60	277.0	179	771.0
Total	438	2,020.5	361	1,502.1	407	1,904.2	319	1,436.3	217	1,059.3	421	1,385.6

FTP = Fast-Track Program, SMEs = small and medium-sized enterprises, W = Korean won.
Source: Industrial Bank of Korea.

Table 12: Existing Corporate Rehabilitation Support Programs

	2017		2018		2019		2020		2021		2022	
	No. of SMEs	Amount (W billion)	No. of SMEs	Amount (W billion)	No. of SMEs	Amount (W billion)	No. of SMEs	Amount (W billion)	No. of SMEs	Amount (W billion)	No. of SMEs	Amount (W billion)
Change-Up	464	2,321.3	419	2,201.3	397	2,098.2	336	1,701.2	243	1,367.2	307	1,224.1
Fast-Track	135	631.5	172	757.1	249	1,177.8	259	1,384.2	246	1,404.0	204	1,221.5
Pre-FTP	107	540.9	62	297.3	56	241.3	120	585.2	134	664.6	242	1,106.7
Total	706	3,493.8	653	3,255.7	702	3,517	715	3,671	623	3,435.7	753	3,552.3

FTP = Fast-Track Program, SMEs = small and medium-sized enterprises, W = Korean won.
Source: Industrial Bank of Korea.

This rehabilitation program was initiated in 1999 by a couple of state-owned banks, including IBK, but has spread to all commercial banks in the country. The Pre-FTP, still only adopted by IBK, is a preemptive program for SMEs before reaching Fast-Track status, and the graduation rates of Fast-Track and pre-FTP are higher than that of Change-Up.[23] Sharing and monitoring financial statements and business status information with major banks on companies at risk of insolvency by dividing them into work-out or fast-track stages is helpful to identify and support the amount of funds essential among the ever-present excess fund demands of companies. Moreover, IBK has installed a pre-fast track step prior to these two steps to monitor corporate capital demand more closely and, if necessary, provide additional funding to SMEs alone without consultation with the major bank.

---

[23] The graduation rate refers to the rate of returned-to-normal companies among companies subject to the rehabilitation support programs.

Table 13 shows graduation rates for all three rehabilitation programs and Table 14 for the other two categories, excluding the Change-Up program (so-called work-out in the Republic of Korea). Unlike other banks, Pre-FTP is a preemptive measure only of IBK. Table 14 shows that the average graduation rate from 2015 to 2019 is 3.3 percentage points higher than that in Table 13 (e.g., 58.2% versus 61.5%). This proves that IBK is proactively increasing the effectiveness of the rehabilitation program through Pre-FTP as well as its own specialty. The IBK's rehabilitation program was able to raise the SME rehabilitation rate, not bankruptcy, by actively implementing interest rate reduction, deferment of principal repayments, and additional operating fund support when there was a possibility of rehabilitation among SMEs showing signs of insolvency.

Table 13: Graduation Rates of Industrial Bank of Korea for all Rehabilitation Support Programs

	2015		2016		2017		2018		2019	
	No. of SMEs	Amount (W billion)	No. of SMEs	Amount (W billion)	No. of SMEs	Amount (W billion)	No. of SMEs	Amount (W billion)	No. of SMEs	Amount (W billion)
Graduation	181	479.1	216	738.6	219	576.1	154	491.0	102	358.0
Dropout	147	533.2	148	665.0	122	386.2	91	344.1	104	358.0
Graduation Rate (%)	55.2		59.3		64.2		62.9		49.5	
Industry Graduation Rate (%)	36.4		30.0		15.4		no data		no data	

SMEs = small and medium-sized enterprises, W = Korean won.
Source: Industrial Bank of Korea, and Korea Institute of Finance (only for the industry graduation rate).

Table 14: Subcategory of Graduation Rates of Industrial Bank of Korea for Fast-Track Program+ Pre-fast-Track Program

	2015		2016		2017		2018		2019	
	No. of SMEs	Amount (W billion)	No. of SMEs	Amount (W billion)	No. of SMEs	Amount (W billion)	No. of SMEs	Amount (W billion)	No. of SMEs	Amount (W billion)
Graduation	85	138.6	235	624.0	60	357.4	108	497.7	85	401.8
Dropout	62	21.1	67	216.0	55	315.8	61	344.1	67	212.5
Graduation Rate (%)	57.8		77.8		52.2		63.9		55.9	

SMEs = small and medium-sized enterprises, W = Korean won.
Source: Industrial Bank of Korea.

In addition, the possibility of SME insolvency widened in the wake of other banks urging principal repayment during a financial crisis, such as in 2008, while IBK held to its motto that it does not "take away umbrellas when it rains." This pattern helped overcome SME difficulties. As such result, IBK achieved a graduation rate of 59.6% from 2015 to 2017, more than double the 27.3% average of the overall banking industry for companies with restructuring contracts, in an evaluation from the Korea Institute of Finance (Table 13) (Koo and Kim 2019). In 2017, the most recent available year that can compare graduation rates between the Korea Institute of Finance report (available until 2017) and this paper, the graduation rate from the rehabilitation program of the entire domestic banking sector was 15.4%, while the IBK was 64.2% (Table 13), much higher. By industry, the graduation rate for SMEs in apparel, rubber plastics, and assembly metals exceeds 60%, but the rate for SMEs in the automobile and shipbuilding sectors is less than 50%.

V — Small and Medium-Sized Enterprise Public Loan Guarantees: The Case of the U.S. Small Business Administration

During the past 30 years, governments around the world have increasingly turned to public credit guarantees as the preferred tool for increasing the availability of credit for SMEs unable to obtain credit from commercial banks and other sources of formal finance. A credit guarantee is a legal contract by which a third party, known as the guarantor, promises to repay part or all of the amount of a loan to a lender should the borrower default. In essence, the guarantor is offering the lender its credit quality in place of the credit quality of the actual borrower.

Beck, Klapper, and Mendoza (2008) examine credit-guarantee schemes in 46 countries, both developed and developing. They conclude that credit-guarantee schemes have become policymakers' preferred tool for improving loan availability, particularly for credit-constrained groups like small and new businesses. Gozzi and Schmukler (2016) review the use of credit-guarantee schemes around the world as a tool for expanding access to credit for MSMEs. They report increasing use of credit-guarantee programs following the global financial crisis of 2008–2009. Existing programs were expanded and new programs were created where none previously existed.

Given this new attention to credit-guarantee programs, it is instructive to look at the government-sponsored entity that has operated some of the earliest and largest such programs—the U.S. Small Business Administration (SBA). The SBA is a US-government agency established to strengthen the US economy and create jobs by assisting small businesses through the provisioning of "counseling, capital, and contracting expertise as the nation's only go-to resource and voice for small businesses."[24]

History, Mission, and Objectives

The SBA is an independent agency that was established by the Small Business Act of 1953 (P.L. 83–163). It was established as a separate organization with the exclusive purpose of assisting, advising, and defending the interests of small businesses, including the preservation of their rights to a fair share of government contracts and sales of surplus property.[25] The SBA Act dissolved the Reconstruction Finance Corporation, which was established during the Great Depression to provide credit to businesses of all sizes, but became mired in charges of cronyism and political favoritism regarding its operation. In its place, the SBA Act authorized the creation of the SBA to assume some functions of the Reconstruction Finance Corporation.

---

[24] See "About SBA" at https://www.sba.gov/about-sba.
[25] Small Business Act (Public Law 85–536, as amended).

The SBA's mission is to "maintain and strengthen the nation's economy by enabling the establishment and vitality of small businesses and by assisting in the economic recovery of communities after disasters." SBA activities are designed to fulfill its 4 strategic goals and 10 strategic objectives (Figure 12).

> The first goal is to support small-business revenue and growth, with three objectives: (i) enhance capital access, (ii) assist small-business exporters in dominating international marketplaces, and (iii) ensure federal contract and innovation set-aside goals are met or exceeded.
> The second goal is to build healthy entrepreneurial ecosystems and create business-friendly environments, under which there are three objectives: (i) develop small businesses through technical assistance, (ii) build healthy entrepreneurial ecosystems, and (iii) create a small-business-friendly environment.
> The third goal is to restore small businesses and communities after disasters, under which there is one objective: to deploy disaster assistance effectively and efficiently.
> The fourth and final goal is to increase SBA's capacity to serve small businesses, under which there are three objectives: (i) to ensure effective and efficient management of agency resources, (ii) to build a high-performing workforce, and (iii) to deploy cost-effective technology and enterprise-wide information-system modernization (SBA 2020a).

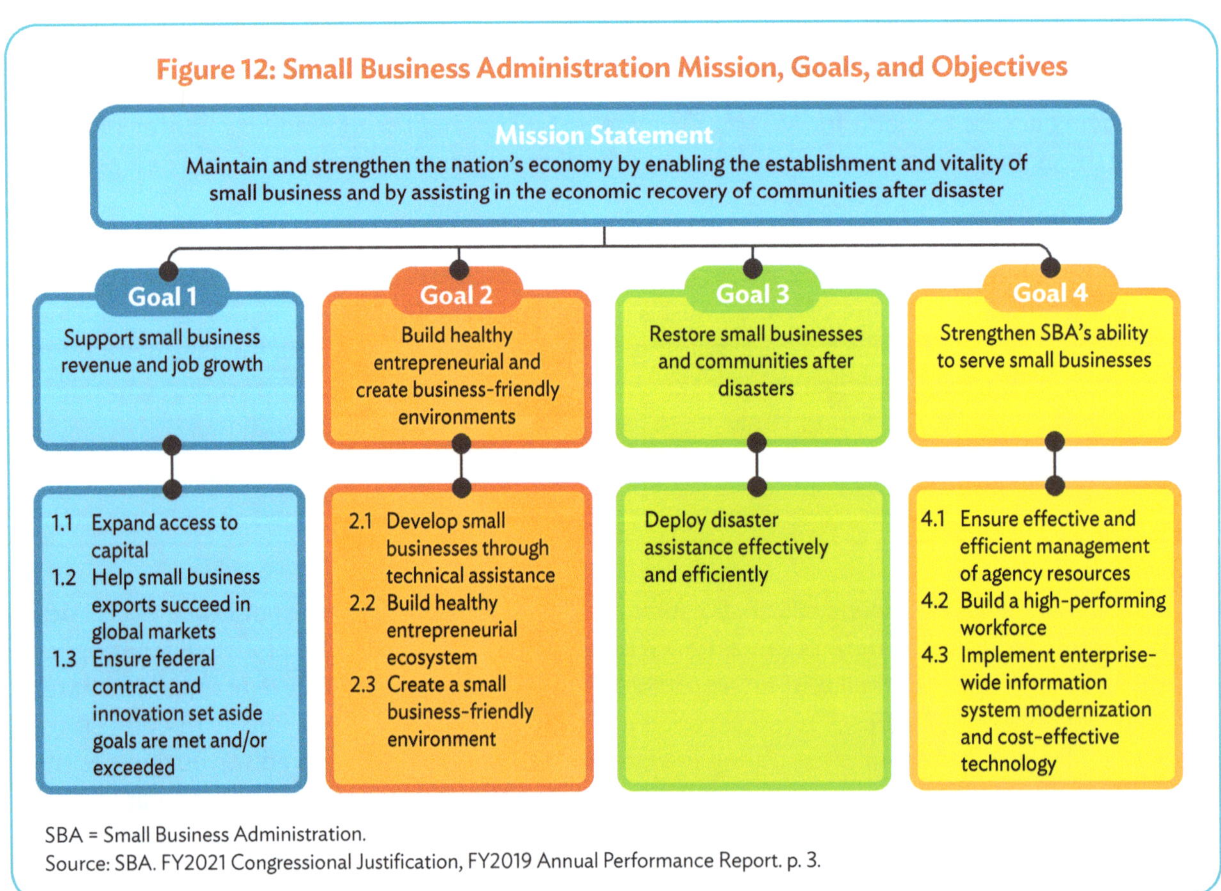

SBA = Small Business Administration.
Source: SBA. FY2021 Congressional Justification, FY2019 Annual Performance Report. p. 3.

The SBA administers a number of programs to support small businesses. These include loan-guarantee programs designed to increase access to private banking sector, venture capital programs to increase access to private-sector equity; contracting programs to improve access to federal contracts; direct lending programs to assist businesses, homeowners, and renters in recovering from disasters triggered by natural hazards; and training programs to support in the establishment and growth of businesses (Congressional Research Service 2019). The SBA's flagship program is its 7(a) loan-guarantee program, which was historically scaled up during 2020 in a response to the COVID-19 pandemic's economic effects. For fiscal year 2020, the SBA's estimated budget was $998.5 million (Table 15).

Table 15: Small Business Administration Budget Fiscal, Year 2020

Program Category	Authorization ($ million)	Ratio (%)
Salaries and expenses	270.2	27.1
Entrepreneurial development programs	261.0	26.1
Business loan program	259.2	26.0
Administration	155.2	15.5
Loan subsidy - guaranteed loan	99.0	9.9
Loan subsidy - microloan	5.0	0.5
Disaster loan programs	177.1	17.7
Inspector general	21.9	2.2
Office of advocacy	9.1	0.9
Total	998.5	100

SBA = Small Business Administration.
Source: SBA. Performance Plan, Budget, and Report, FY2019 Annual Performance Report.

Supplemental appropriations for programs related to COVID-19 totaled to nearly $752 billion, primarily for funding the Paycheck Protection Program amounting to around $525 billion, a program that provides a direct incentive for small businesses to keep their workers on the payroll.[26] One sees that the SBA's disaster loan programs (see Box 3) budget was scaled up from $10 million in 2019 to $177.1 million in 2020 to fund the new COVID-related lending initiatives, illustrating the importance and versatility of the agency.[27]

---

[26] 2020 Agency Financial Report. Summary of Covid-19 Financial Impacts.
[27] In 2018, there was no allotted budget for the disaster loan programs. The program budget was $168.1 million in 2021 and $178 million in 2022: see 2018–2022 SBA Congressional Budget Justification. https://www.sba.gov/document/report-congressional-budget-justification-annual-performance-report.

Box 3: Primer on the Small Business Administration's Principal Programs on Disaster Assistance

Disaster Assistance—The U.S. Small Business Administration (SBA) is the Federal government's primary source of financing for the long-term repair and rebuilding of disaster-damaged private property for homeowners, renters, businesses of all sizes, and private nonprofit organizations. It is the only form of SBA assistance that is not limited to small businesses. The SBA disaster loan can be used for Losses not covered by insurance or funding from the Federal Emergency Management Agency for both personal and business and for Business operating expenses that could have been met had the disaster not occurred.

Paycheck Protection Program—The CARES Act established this loan of up to $10 million designed to provide a direct incentive for small businesses to keep their workers on the payroll. The loan may be fully forgiven if the funds are used for payroll costs, interest on mortgages, rent, and utilities. The program ended 31 May 2021.

COVID EIDL Loans—The CARES Act modified the existing Economic Injury Disaster Loan (EIDL) within the Disaster Assistance program. In response to the coronavirus disease (COVID-19) pandemic, small businesses owners, including agricultural cooperatives and nonprofit organizations, can apply for these loans, which go up to $2 million and must be repaid.

COVID EIDL Advance—These grants, up to $10,000 in value, went to small businesses that also applied for COVID EIDL Loans and are not repaid.

Restaurant Revitalization Fund—The American Rescue Plan Act established the fund to provide funding to help restaurants and other eligible businesses keep their doors open. This program provides restaurants with funding equal to their pandemic-related revenue loss up to $10 million per business and no more than $5 million per physical location. Recipients are not required to repay the funding if funds are spent for eligible uses.

Shuttered Venue Operators Grants—The Economic Aid to Hard-Hit Small Businesses, Nonprofits, and Venues Act established these grants to support shuttered venues because of the COVID-19 pandemic. Recipients are not required to repay the grants if funds are spent for eligible uses within established timeframes.

Source: 2022 SBA Financial Agency Report, Primer of the SBA`s Principal Programs.

Its major goal is to make capital more accessible to small firms through programs that encourage financial institutions and investors to provide loans and equity to small enterprises that would otherwise be neglected due to their perceived risks.

While the SBA's disaster-relief program does allow it to provide direct loans to small companies, its flagship programs incentivize creditors and investors through partial loan guarantees (7(a) loan guarantee programs) and investment programs (Small Business Investment Company Program).

Key Programs and Products

The SBA offers two major loan-guarantee programs: 7(a), and 504, these providing traditional lenders that have been qualified by the SBA with guarantees of partial repayment should there be a default by the borrower.

7(a) General Business Loan-Guaranty Program. The SBA's primary loan program is the 7(a) General Business Loan-Guaranty Program. It is utilized by small businesses to meet various financing needs, such as working capital, purchase of equipment and real estate, leasehold improvements, and inventory. The standard 7(a) program accounts for about two-thirds of the SBA's guarantee programs and guarantees loans up to $150,000 with an 85% guarantee and loans over $150,000 with a 75% guarantee, up to a maximum of $5 million. Negotiations between lenders and borrowers over interest rates are subject to an SBA maximum. Lenders are not required to take collateral for loans up to $25,000. For loans in excess of $350,000, the SBA requires that the lender collateralize the loan to the maximum extent possible up to the loan amount.[28] Borrower eligibility for almost all SBA programs, including 7(a), are dictated by small-business size.[29] There also is a 7(a) "small loan" with a maximum amount of $350,000. Again, there is an 85% guarantee for loans up to $150,000 and 75% for larger loans. Collateral requirements are largely the same. Table 16 shows the subsidy and fee structure of the 7(a) program.

In FY2019, the SBA authorized 58,006 7(a) and 504 loans totaling $28.1 billion through 1,708 7(a) lenders and 212 Certified Development Companies to small firms.

Table 16: 7(a) Loan Program Subsidy and Fee Structure

	Current	FY2021 Request
Subsidy rate	5 basis points (bps) ($15 million in subsidy appropriation needed for $30 billion program level)	0 bps
Fee structure	**Up-front fee:** • Loans <= $150,000: 2.0% (1.5% remitted to Small Business Administration) • $150,000 < Loans <= $700,000: 3.0% • Loans > $700,000: 3.50% • Additional 0.25% fee for any guaranteed amount over $1 million • Loan term less than 1 year: 0.25% • Export Working Capital Program loans, 13–24 month maturity: 0.525% • Export Working Capital Program loans, 25–36 month maturity: 0.80% **Ongoing fee:** 55 bps	**Administrative fee:** • $0.16 per every hundred dollars approved based on $30 billion in lending **Up-front fee:** • Loans <= $150,000: 2.0% (1.5% remitted to SBA) • $150,000 < Loans <= $700,000: 3.0% Loans > $700,000: 3.64% • Additional 0.25% fee for any guaranteed amount over $1 million • Loan term less than 1 year: 0.25% • Export Working Capital Program loans, 13–24 month maturity: 0.525% • Export Working Capital Program loans, 25–36 month maturity: 0.80% **Ongoing fee:** 55 bps • Up-front fee waived for SBA Express loans to veterans

Source: U.S. Small Business Administration (SBA). SBA FY2021 Congressional Justification, FY2019 Annual Performance Report. p. 29.

---

[28] See U.S. Small Business Administration. Types of 7(a) loans. https://www.sba.gov/partners/lenders/7a-loan-program/types-7a-loans.

[29] See the SBA's Tables of Size Standards for complete details of SBA small business size standards. https://www.sba.gov/document/support-table-size-standards.

504 Certified Development Company Loan Guarantee Program. The SBA's 504 loan guarantee program was designed to help businesses buy fixed assets for modernization or growth at a fixed rate for a lengthy period of time. These loans are only available from Certified Development Companies (with whom the SBA partners to provide such credit). Certified Development Companies are nonprofit corporations that make 504 loans and are backed by SBA-guaranteed debentures to encourage economic development in their communities. There were 260 Certified Development Companies operating in the US as of 2020, each of which has a specific geographic region, often the state in which it is headquartered.

A typical 504 project involves a senior first-lien loan from a private lender, a second-lien loan from a Certified Development Company guaranteed by the SBA, and equity made by the borrower. The typical financing structure for a 504 loan is:

> Private-sector lender: 50% (first-lien position)
> Certified Development Company lender: 40% (second-lien position)
> Borrower: 10% (equity contribution)

The maximum loan amount under the 504 program is $16.5 million for each small business, with loans of up to $5 million and $5.5 million each allowed for manufacturing or energy-efficient projects. The term of the loan can be 10, 20, or 25 years. While the 7(a) program also accommodates real-asset acquisitions with the same maturity, the 504 offers fixed interest rates and guarantee fees are only applied to the private lender's first lien position (50% of loan amount) against 7(a), which charges a fee on its guarantee on 75%–85% of the loan amount.[30] Table 17 shows the subsidy and fee structure of the 504 program.

Table 17: 504 Loan Program Subsidy and Fee Structure

	Current Law Scenario	FY2021 Request
504 certified development company	**Up-front fee:** 50 basis points (bps) **Ongoing fee:** 45.17 bps	**Administrative fee:** • $0.24 per $100 approved based on $7.5 billion in lending **Up-front fee:** 50 bps **Ongoing fee:** 45.30 bps
504 Refinancing	**Up-front fee:** 50 bps **Ongoing fee:** 48.65 bps	**Administrative fee:** • $0.24 per every hundred dollars approved based on $1 billion in lending **Up-front fee:** 50 bps **Ongoing fee:** 48.75 bps

FY = fiscal year.
Source: U.S. Small Business Administration. SBA FY2021 Congressional Justification, FY2019 Annual Performance Report. p. 32.

---

[30] See Office of Financial Assistance: Resources at https://www.sba.gov/offices/headquarters/ofa/resources/4049.

Table 18: Summary of the Microloan Program's Key Features

Key Feature	Program Summary
Use of proceeds	Working capital and acquisition of materials, supplies, furniture, fixtures, and equipment. Loans cannot be made to acquire land or property.
Maximum loan amount	$50,000
Maturity	Up to 7 years.
Maximum interest rates	The Small Business Administration (SBA) charges intermediaries an interest rate that is based on the 5-year Treasury rate, adjusted to the nearest 1/8% (called the base rate), less 1.25% if the intermediary maintains a historic portfolio of microloans averaging more than $10,000 and less 2.0% if the intermediary maintains a historic portfolio of microloans averaging $10,000 or less. The base rate, after adjustment, is called the intermediary's cost of funds—which is initially calculated 1 year from the date of the note and reviewed annually and adjusted as necessary. On loans of more than $10,000, the maximum interest rate that can be charged to the borrower is the interest rate charged by the SBA on the loan to the intermediary, plus 7.75%. On loans of $10,000 or less, the maximum interest rate that can be charged to the borrower is the interest charged by the SBA on the loan to the intermediary, plus 8.5%. Rates are negotiated between the borrower and the intermediary and typically range from 7% to 9%.
Guaranty fees	The SBA does not charge intermediaries up-front or ongoing service fees under the Microloan program.
Job creation requirements	No job creation requirements

Source: *Small Business Administration: A Primer on Programs and Funding* (6 October 2020). p. 16.

Microloan Program. The SBA's Microloan program offers loans up to $50,000 to help the start-up and growth of small enterprises and select nonprofit childcare centers. The average microloan is about $13,000, the maximum loan maturity is 6 years, and loan rates have been in the range of 8%–13% a year. The average loan amount was $14,735 in FY2019, with an average loan rate of 7.5%. Working capital, inventory, furniture or fixtures, and machinery or equipment can all be financed using microloans, but they cannot be employed to pay off debt or purchase property.

The Small Business Reauthorization Act of 1997 made the Microloan program permanent after it received authorization in 1991 as a 5-year pilot program. It went into operation in 1992. The initiative focuses on start-ups in underserved markets with little to no credit history, particularly minority- and female-owned businesses and those in remote places. Table 18 summarizes the key features of the program.

The Microloan program provides direct loans to nonprofit lenders and they, in turn, make loans to small businesses in amounts of $50,000 or less. Microlenders provide technical assistance (e.g., marketing and management) to both prospective and definite borrowers. Additionally, to help offset the expense of providing micro-borrowers with business training services, SBA offers grants to intermediary lenders of up to 25% of the loan amount. The combination of debt financing, technical assistance, and training helps build up the capacity of the micro-borrowers so that they can improve operations, grow their businesses, support job creation and retention, and earn a profit. Through 144 microlenders, 5,532 small enterprises received microloans totaling $81.5 million for FY2019, sustaining 21,235 jobs. Table 19 presents select microloan performance indicators for fiscal years 2014–2019 and targets for FY2020–2021.[31]

Table 19: Microloan Performance Indicators, 2014–2021

		2014	2015	2016	2017	2018	2019	2020	2021
Number of small businesses assisted by microloans	Target	3,650	3,650	3,650	4,000	4,500	4,500	5,600	5,650
	Actual	3,917	3,694	4,506	4,958	5,457	5,532	5,892	4,514
	Variance	7%	1%	23%	24%	21%	23%	5%	−20%

Additional Information: Microloan Intermediaries must make at least 10 microloans per year to meet performance levels. New lenders are added as qualified applications are received for communities that show a need for microloan services.

		2014	2015	2016	2017	2018	2019	2020	2021
Loans approved by lenders to micro borrower ($ '000)	Target	45,000	45,000	55,000	62,800	62,800	65,000	82,000	82,500
	Actual	55,478	52,080	61,223	68,518	76,743	81,529	84,985	74,694
	Variance	23%	16%	11%	9%	22%	25%	4%	−10%

Additional Information: These dollars represent those made by the microlender to the borrower.

		2014	2015	2016	2017	2018	2019	2020	2021
Number of jobs supported by microloans	Target	12,750	12,750	15,000	15,900	17,500	17,500	21,500	21,750
	Actual	15,880	16,600	17,573	18,531	20,486	21,235	24,596	17,531
	Variance	25%	30%	17%	17%	17%	21%	14%	−19%

Additional Information: The Small Business Administration (SBA) tracks the number of jobs supported from each loan. The decrease in FY2021 actuals from the prior year stemmed from intermediaries shifting their focus to other funding resources better suited to their borrower's needs for pandemic relief.

		2014	2015	2016	2017	2018	2019	2020	2021
Number of grant-eligible microlenders	Target	135	135	135	140	140	144	150	155
	Actual	137	137	140	144	147	144	155	140
	Variance	1%	1%	4%	3%	5%	0%	3%	−7%

Additional Information: The SBA tracks the number of grant-eligible microlenders. Grant-eligible microlenders are lenders who comply with program requirements.

FY = fiscal year.
Source: U.S. Small Business Administration. SBA FY2021 Congressional Justification, FY2019 Annual Performance Report. pp. 35–36.

---

[31]   See U.S. Small Business Administration. Performance Plan, Budget, and Report, FY 2019–FY 2023 Annual Performance Report.

Disaster Assistance Program. The Disaster Assistance Program is the only form of SBA assistance made available to all businesses, and provides direct SBA loans to businesses of all sizes as well as households affected by disasters triggered by natural hazards such as hurricanes, floods, earthquakes, and others. About 80% of these loans are made to individuals and households, with the remainder going to small businesses.

Loans are made available for property damage and economic injury costs. Property-damage loans are estimated by "loss verifiers" and include costs of repair and/or replacement of real assets net of the insured amount. Economic-injury loans are made available for eligible small businesses within the declared disaster area and have sustained significant economic injury as a result of the disaster. Economic disaster loans are capped at $2 million.[32]

Table 20: Disaster Relief Loans, 2011–2019

Year	Number	Amount ($ billion)	Average Amount ($)
2011	13,644	0.78	57,373
2012	15,330	0.75	48,727
2013	46,826	2.92	62,317
2014	6,244	0.43	68,326
2015	11,448	0.41	36,070
2016	25,235	1.45	57,295
2017	27,264	1.77	64,771
2018	140,249	7.39	52,726
2019	42,399	2.45	57,678

Source: U.S. Small Business Administration. Small Business Administration Loan Program Performance (31 March 2020).

As shown in Table 20, the number of disaster relief loans fluctuated widely during 2011–2019 from a low of 6,244 in FY2014 to a high of 140,249 in FY2018. The gross approval amounts showed similar fluctuations, from a low of $0.41 billion in FY2015 to a high of $7.39 billion in FY2018. The average loan amount was much more stable, ranging from $36,070 in FY2015 to $68,326 in FY2014.

Small Business Investment Company Program. The Small Business Investment Company (SBIC) Program was established in 1958 to bridge the gap between the financial needs of businesses and the available funds from traditional sources of finance. Small businesses in the US now have access to funding worth billions of dollars thanks to the initiative, covering a wide range of sectors.

---

[32] U.S. Small Business Administration. Disaster Loan Assistance. https://disasterloan.sba.gov/ela/Information/BusinessPhysicalLoans (accessed 28 November 2020).

These results were achieved through a public–private partnership that leveraged the US government's "full faith" and credit to increase the accessible funding for private sector investments to small businesses. The SBA provides funding to SBICs through the issuance of taxpayer-backed debentures. These funds are augmented with capital raised by privately and publicly managed investment funds that pool investments from private investors, such as banks, pension funds, or wealthy individuals.

A license to run an SBIC is provided to qualified fund managers who pass the SBA's stringent application procedure. SBA will pledge up to $2 of debt for every $1 the fund earns from investors, up to a maximum of $175 million. The SBIC then invests this combined fund in small enterprises that meet certain criteria (Figure 13). The SBIC and small businesses agree on loan conditions in accordance with the SBIC Program's standards. The SBIC's main features are presented in Table 21.

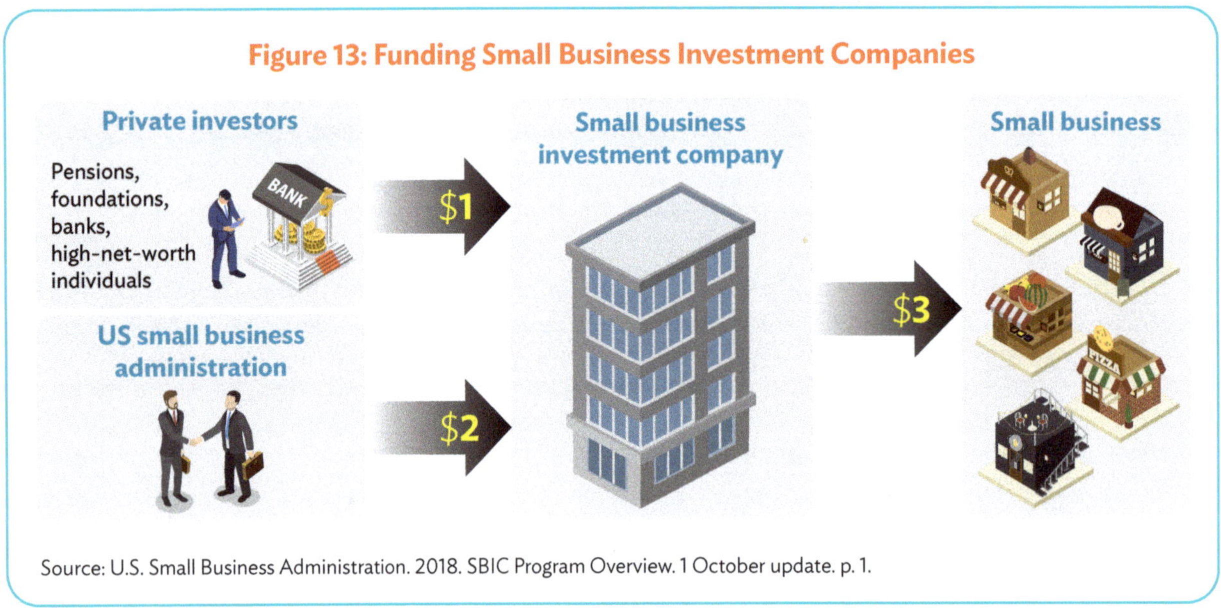

Source: U.S. Small Business Administration. 2018. SBIC Program Overview. 1 October update. p. 1.

Table 21: Small Business Investment Company Program Key Features

Key Feature	Program Summary
Use of proceeds	To purchase small business equity securities, make loans to small businesses, purchase debt securities from small businesses, and provide, subject to limitations, small businesses a guarantee of their monetary obligations to creditors not associated with the Small Business Investment Company (SBIC).
Maximum leverage amount	A licensed SBIC in good standing with a demonstrated need for funds may apply to the SBA for financial assistance (called leverage) of up to 300% of its private capital. However, most SBICs are approved for a maximum of 200% of their private capital, and no fund management team may exceed the allowable maximum amount of leverage, currently $175 million per SBIC and $350 million for two or more licenses under common control.

continued on next page

Table 21 *continued*

Key Feature	Program Summary
Maturity	SBA-guaranteed debenture participation certificates can have a term of up to 15 years, although currently only one outstanding SBA-guaranteed debenture participation certificate has a term exceeding 10 years and all recent public offerings have specified a term of 10 years. SBA-guaranteed debentures provide for semiannual interest payments and a lump sum principal payment to investors at maturity. SBICs are allowed to prepay SBA-guaranteed debentures without penalty. However, a SBA-guaranteed debenture must be prepaid in whole and not in part and can only be prepaid on a semiannual payment date. Also, low-to-moderate income area debentures are available in two maturities, for 5 years and 10 years (plus the stub period).
Maximum interest rates	The debenture's coupon (interest) rate is determined by market conditions and the interest rate of 10-year Treasury securities at the time of the sale.
Guaranty fees	The SBA requires the SBIC to pay a 3% origination fee for each debenture issued (1% at commitment and 2% at draw), an annual fee on the leverage drawn, which is fixed at the time of the leverage commitment, and other administrative and underwriting fees, which are adjusted annually.
Job creation requirements	No job creation requirements.
Use of proceeds	To purchase small business equity securities, make loans to small businesses, purchase debt securities from small businesses, and provide, subject to limitations, small businesses a guarantee of their monetary obligations to creditors not associated with the SBIC.

SBIC = small business investment company.
Source: U.S. Small Business Administration (SBA). 2020. *Small Business Administration: A Primer on Programs and Funding.* p. 32.

The goal of the SBIC Program is to boost the flow of long-term loans and private equity capital to small enterprises, which are essential for a company's development, expansion, and modernization when such funding is scarce. It was founded in 1958 and has lent more than $67 billion since its inception. It was allowed to lend up to $4 billion annually as of 2020, managed $26 billion in assets, and provided loans to 303 active SBICs.[33]

The SBA provides funding of $1.93 billion in FY2019 through the issuance of debentures to SBICs, and they invested another $3.94 billion from private sources of capital for a total of nearly $6 billion in financing for 1,191 small enterprises.[34]

Table 22 provides performance information on the program for FY2016–FY2022.The total SBIC financing amount in 2022 reached at around $7.8 billion with straight debt type of financing that has the biggest share amounting to around $5 billion. It was quite notable that in FY2021, bouncing back from the pandemic in 2020, SBA has increased its total financing by 31%, the number of companies financed increased by 90% and the number of jobs generated or sustained increased by 28%.

---

[33] See U.S. Small Business Administration. SBIC Program Overview. https://www.sba.gov/document/support--sbic-program-overview.
[34] U.S. Small Business Administration. SBIC Program Overview. https://www.sba.gov/document/support--sbic-program-overview (accessed 28 November 2020).

Table 22: Small Business Investment Company Program Performance

SBIC Program	2016	2017	2018	2019	2020	2021	2022
Financing amount ($ million)	5,991.7	5,727.3	5,502.6	5,865.7	4,885.0	7,103.7	7,862.4
Type of financing ($ million)							
Straight debt	3,791.7	3,720.2	3,543.0	3,594.4	3,026.8	4,540.3	5,054.2
Debt with equity features	1,157.1	859.8	807.3	792	648.7	802.9	888.5
Equity only	1,042.9	1,147.4	1,152.2	1,479.3	1,209.5	1,760.5	1,919.6
No. of companies financed	1,201	1,077	1,151	1,191	1,063	10,580	1,217
Special competitive opportunity gap business	332	308	315	292	262	253	326
Business located in low moderate-income areas	284	262	265	245	224	200	263
Woman-, minority-, veteran- owned businesses	61	68	66	59	55	75	82
No. of jobs created or sustained	122,382	112,865	106,021	111,201	91,559	126,431	129,098

SBIC = Small Business Investment Company.
Source: U.S. Small Business Administration. SBIC Program Overview for the quarter ending 31 March 2023.

Economic Impact

Small businesses (firms employing fewer than 500 employees) play a major role in the US economy, contributing 43.5% to the 2014 GDP (Kobe and Schwinn 2018). Small businesses represent 99.9% of all businesses (30.7 million firms) and employ 47.3% of the total US workforce (59.9 million employees) (SBA 2019). Additionally, small businesses created more jobs compared to large firms, accounting for 9.3 million net new private sector jobs from 2005 to 2019 (64% of the total) (SBA 2020b).

As a significant driver of the US economy, policymakers need to create a conducive environment for the survival and growth of small businesses. For small companies to succeed in the long run, having access to capital is essential as many are facing constrained access to formal credit compared to larger firms. Business start-ups and businesses owned by minorities face difficulties in acquiring loans due to lack of established credit scores and social dynamics (SBA 2017). For example, during the third quarter of 2017, there were 241,000 establishment start-ups, but 226,000 establishment exits (SBA 2019). Banks are the leading external source of funding for small businesses but data from the Federal Deposit Insurance Corporation indicate that the amount of small-business, lending by commercial banks has decreased since its peak in 2008. As shown in Figure 14, the amount of small-business lending remained below its 2008 peak of $710 billion throughout 2008–2019, while the amount of big-business lending almost doubled from $1.56 trillion to $2.75 trillion.

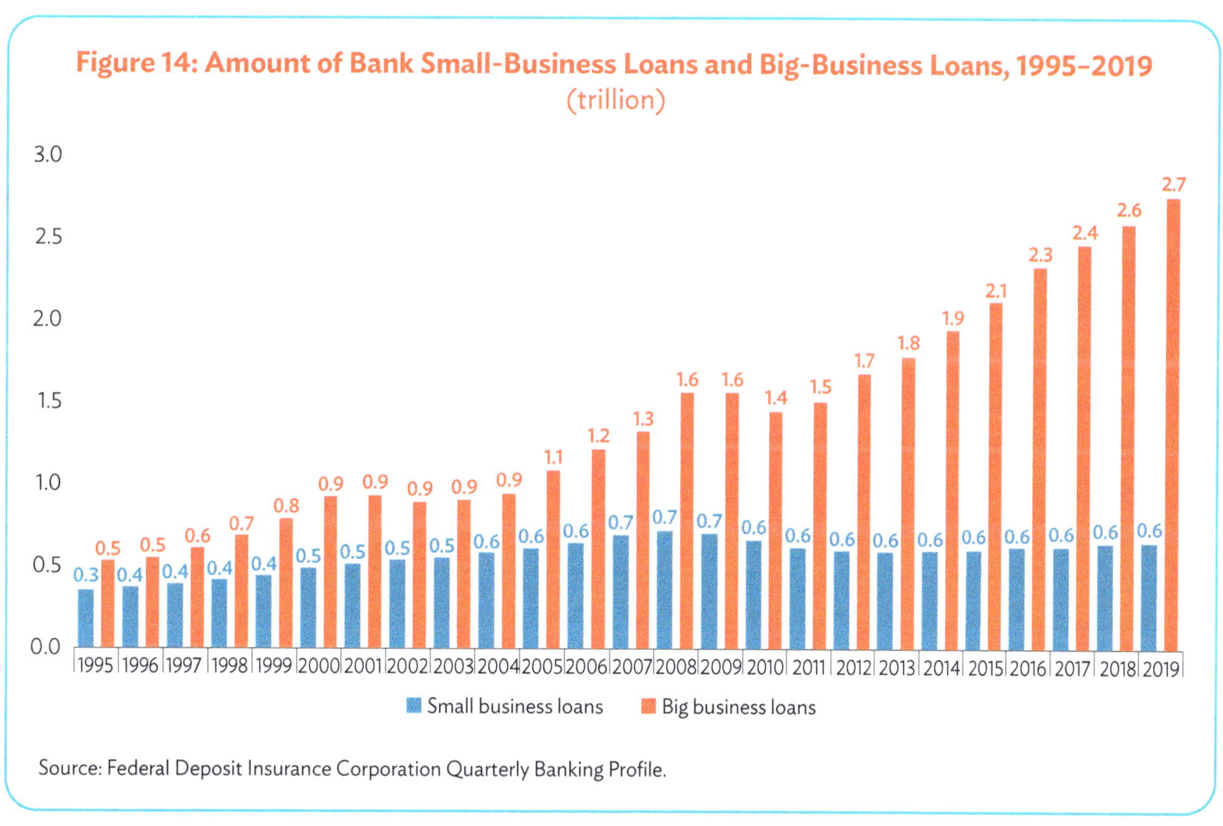

Source: Federal Deposit Insurance Corporation Quarterly Banking Profile.

An important contributing factor to the decline in small-business bank credit is the decrease in the number of small banks as the US banking industry has experienced large-scale consolidation. From 2000 to 2019, the number of US commercial banks decreased from 8,315 to only 4,136.[35] Traditionally, smaller banks have been more invested in small business lending due to their localized setting and lending regulations. For example, approval rates are higher for small banks (50.6%) against large banks (28.2%) (SBA 2020b). As of 2016, small banks (less than $10 billion assets) held 10.2% of their total assets in small business lending in contrast to large banks with 4.8% (Federal Reserve 2017). As of year-end 2022, banks with less than $10 billion in assets accounted for only an average of 18% of industry assets (footnote 35).

Role and Impact of Small Business Administration in Small-Business Financing. Credit-market constraints faced by small businesses highlight the importance of SBA programs in contributing to small-business growth and economic development. The SBA's strategic goals of supporting small-business revenues and job growth specifically target the expansion of capital available to small businesses. During fiscal years 2014–2022, SBA's access to capital programs has contributed to the approval of 17,521,201 small-business loans (Figure 15). During the same period, gross approval amounts totaled to around $1.59 trillion (Figure 16). During FY2022 alone, SBA programs supported actual jobs of around 1.5 million jobs.[36]

---

[35]   Federal Deposit Insurance Corporation. FDIC Annual Historical Bank data. https://banks.data.fdic.gov/explore/historical/ (accessed on 3 July 2023).
[36]   SBA Agency Financial Report FY 2022: Summary of Performance Results.

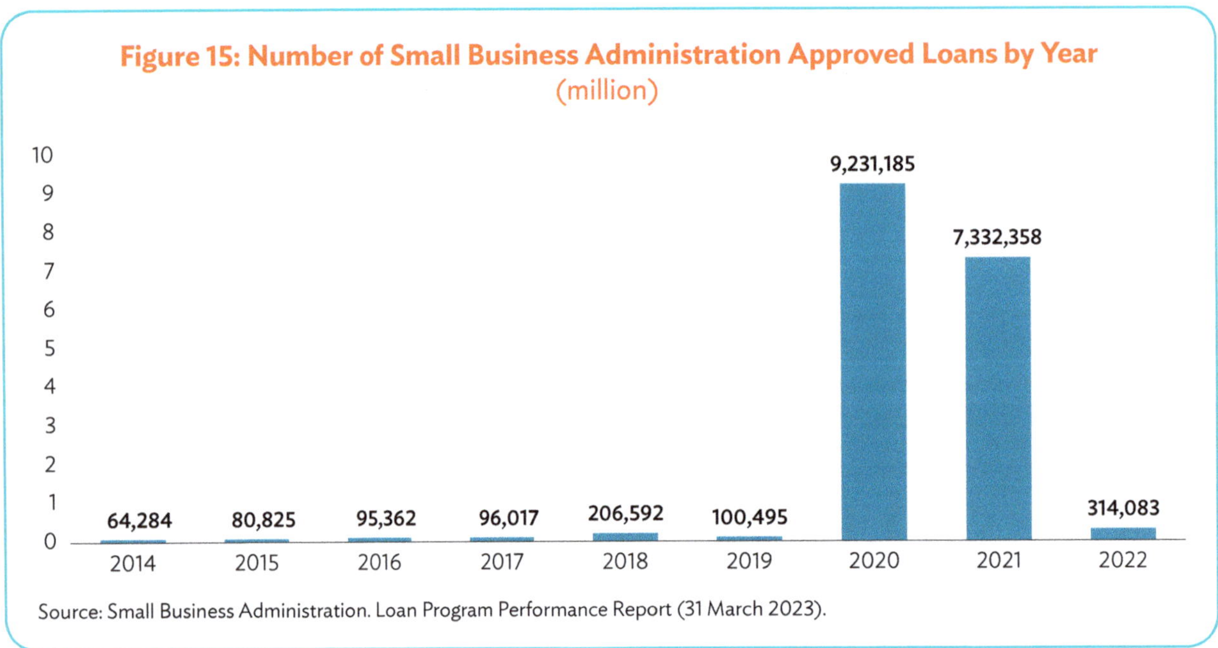

Figure 15: Number of Small Business Administration Approved Loans by Year
(million)

Source: Small Business Administration. Loan Program Performance Report (31 March 2023).

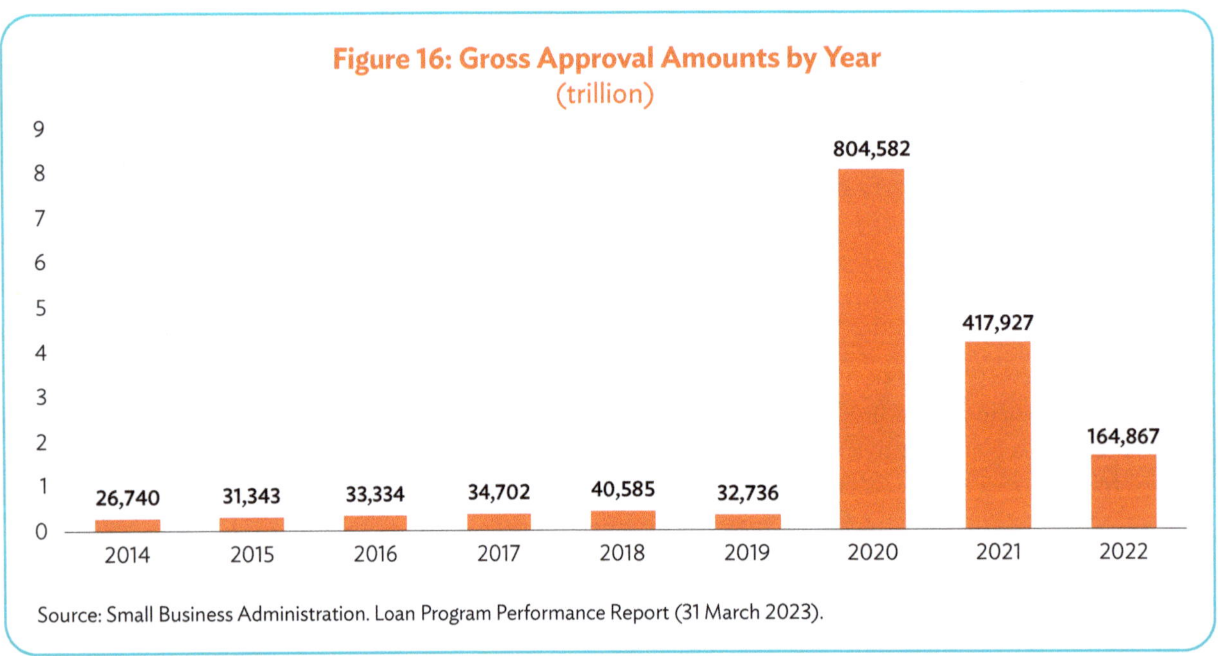

Figure 16: Gross Approval Amounts by Year
(trillion)

Source: Small Business Administration. Loan Program Performance Report (31 March 2023).

Beyond providing access to funding to small businesses, SBA programs have a wider macroeconomic effect as small businesses debt leads to lower failure rates and higher revenues (Cole and Sokolyk 2018). Craig, Jackson, and Thomson (2009) survey the literature on SBA programs and conclude that the evidence shows a small positive impact of SBA programs on economic performance. Empirical literature illustrates that SBA programs have a positive and significant impact on small-business growth (Cortes 2010) and job creation (Armstrong et al. 2014; Brown and Earle 2017; Craig, Jackson and Thomson 2007). In one of the most comprehensive and convincing studies of the impact of SBA programs, Brown and Earle (2017) find that each $1 million in SBA loans led to 3–3.5 new jobs, and that this effect is stronger for younger and larger firms, as well as during periods when local credit conditions are weak. They estimate the taxpayer cost for each new job is less than $25,000. Orzechowski (2019) finds a small, but positive relationship between SBA lending per capita and state employment rates.

Small Business Administration's Role in Crisis Response. Aside from access to capital programs, SBA has played a critical role in delivering crucial support during external shocks such as financial crises and disasters triggered by natural hazards. Small firms were hit hard by the global financial crisis of 2007/08, as banks tightened loans owing to worsening financial conditions. The American Recovery and Reinvestment Act of 2009 utilized the SBA as the main means of response and provided $730 million for SBA programs, including but not restricted to:

(i) $375 million for temporary eliminating fees on SBA-backed loans and increased guarantees from a maximum of 80% to 90%;

(ii) $255 million for a new loan program to assist in small businesses' debt servicing capacity;

(iii) $30 million for expanding SBA's microloan program (Social Security Administration 2009). The program led to a sharp increase in lending, leading to a quicker recovery for SBA-accredited small-business lenders, with loan levels quickly returning to precrisis levels (SBA 2009).

During the COVID-19 pandemic, many small businesses were exposed to government mandates that imposed safety measures to mitigate the spread of the virus. As a result, at the height of the pandemic, many small businesses were forced to stop operations due to mandatory closure of business. The US government signed the Coronavirus Aid, Relief, and Economic Security (CARES) Act on 27 March 2020, releasing $376 billion in relief funds for workers and small businesses to alleviate the strain on these businesses. SBA's Paycheck Protection Program, Economic Injury Disaster Loan, SBA Express Bridge Loans, and SBA Debt Relief were all introduced or revamped to aid the government's efforts to support struggling small companies.

In response to the then-emerging COVID-19 pandemic, the US Congress passed the CARES Act, which was signed into law by President Donald Trump on 27 March 2020. The CARES Act was a $2.2 trillion economic stimulus package to provide fast and substantive economic relief to American families and small businesses adversely affected by COVID-19 and the associated lockdowns of the US economy.

The dilemma facing policymakers was how to quickly and effectively distribute more than half a trillion dollars in funding to America's 30 million+ MSMEs, including proprietors and contract workers, so that they could pay salaries, rent, and other business expenses while millions were effectively forced to shut down by state government edicts. The US Treasury chose to utilize the long-established SBA 7A guaranteed loan program to provide funds to MSMEs through the existing roster of SBA-approved lenders, which would be augmented with thousands of newly approved lenders.

The CARES Act established the Paycheck Protection Program, which was initially authorized to guarantee up to $350 billion in loans to cover payroll costs and certain other business expenses for up to 10 weeks. The program decreed that no collateral or personal guarantees would be required.

The loan program is meant to give small businesses a tangible incentive to retain their employees on the payroll. The SBA guaranteed up to $10 million in loans to qualified enterprises, which were issued by banks and credit unions.

On 23 April 2020, Congress approved a second tranche of funding of $310 billion, plus an additional $50 billion for Economic Injury Disaster Loans and $10 billion for emergency Economic Injury Disaster Loans grants. $60 billion in Paycheck Protection Program funding was set aside for lenders with less than $50 billion in assets. Initially, the window on applications closed on 30 June 2020, when $130 billion in funding remained unclaimed. Congress extended the application deadline to 8 August 2020 in a bill signed by President Trump on 4 July 2020. As of 31 July 2020, the SBA had approved 5,083,585 Paycheck Protection Program loans amounting to $521.39 billion. The program stopped accepting applications as of 8 August 2020.

Small firms as defined by the SBA's size criteria, which vary by industry, are eligible for EIDL. Small farms and small cooperatives are eligible for such loans when the Secretary of Agriculture declares an agriculture production disaster. The loans are also accessible in counties that have been declared disaster areas by the president. These loans are intended to give small businesses operational funds until they are able to recover. The maximum loan amount is $2 million, with terms similar to those for personal and physical-disaster business loans. EIDLs have a maximum maturity of 30 years and have interest rates of 4% or less.[37]

Small businesses and nongovernment organizations affected by COVID-19 can get up to $2 million in working capital loans from the SBA. Small firms pay 3.75% interest on these loans, while nongovernment organizations pay 2.75%. Loan repayment terms range from 1 to 30 years, depending on the applicant. The stimulus program has been modified to include single owners and enterprises with less than 500 employees, and applicants for loans under $200,000 do not need to offer a personal guarantee. Additionally, payments may be deferred for up to 4 years.

Small businesses affected by the COVID-19 pandemic were granted EIDL eligibility by the Coronavirus Preparedness and Response Supplemental Appropriations Act, 2020 (P.L. 116–123). The CARES Act (P.L. 116–136) temporarily extended EIDL eligibility to start-ups, cooperatives, and qualified employee-owned businesses with less than 500 employees, sole proprietors, and independent contractors, for a limited time (until 31 December 2020).

---

[37]   See the Code of Federal Regulations at 13 C.F.R. §123.302.

VI Conclusion

Access to finance remains a fundamental obstacle for developing SMEs, despite that formal SMEs represent well over 90% of all businesses worldwide and account for more than half of global employment. This is true for both emerging and developed economies, with SMEs having restricted access to traditional sources of finance, with limited capital markets and information asymmetry hindering bank engagement.

Many SMEs lack both credible financial records and adequate tangible assets to use as collateral for loans. Furthermore, they frequently lack a guarantee for their debts. At the same time, fixed and variable costs are imposed on formal lenders that offer credit to SMEs by financial regulations and underwriting standards. Even when SMEs are able to acquire formal financing, they are frequently subjected to onerous loan terms, such as excessive interest rates and requests for collateral and personal guarantees, which can put an entrepreneur's whole personal wealth in distress.

Although a number of obstacles prevent SMEs from accessing loans, policymakers can use a few feasible alternatives. Governments can establish a specialized bank that extends financing to SMEs, for example, such as the Republic of Korea has done with the Industrial Bank of Korea. A government entity could also provide direct credit and loan guarantee services to SMEs that apply for credit from traditional financial institutions, such as commercial banks, following the example set by the SBA in the US.

This report has examined how these two cases contributed to broader access to credit. In the Republic of Korea, the Ministry of SMEs and Startups was given the task of creating and implementing government policies to promote firm growth, foster start-ups, and support MSMEs. The Industrial Bank of Korea was set up in 1961 to offer financial services to SMEs with limited resources in markets. Since 1981, it has expanded policy loan provision to SMEs that make intermediate goods for on-selling to big firms and in 1989, it expanded to provide policy loans for small firms with good potential, but fewer than 50 employees. In 1991, it made it possible to lend within certain limits without the need for physical collateral or a joint guarantor.

IBK began growing its nonbanking financial business in 1986, with the introduction of a Korean corporate lease to address the limits of traditional lending to SMEs. In addition to loans, it offers complete support measures such as investor recruiting for SMEs, equity investment decisions, investment and technical assistance, credit reinforcement, and facility lending. It also offers financing and consultations to SMEs at all stages of their development. As of 2022, IBK has a W220.7 trillion ($ 168 billion) portfolio of SME loans for more than 2.1 million SME clients.

In the US, the U.S. Small Business Administration was created in 1953 to aid, counsel, assist, and protect the interests of small business concerns. Its primary goal is to support small-business revenue and growth with the objective of expanding access to capital. The SBA's flagship program is its 7(a) loan guarantee program, which is typically utilized by firms to address a variety of needs for their current operations, including the acquisition of equipment, working capital, leasehold improvements, inventory, or real estate. Its innovative Small Business Investment Company (SBIC) Program is a public–private partnership that employs the US government's full faith and credit to leverage private-sector investment capital from privately and publicly managed investment funds and make it available to US SMEs.

As of 2019, the unpaid principal balances of the SBA's four major programs totaled more than $141 billion, with $33 billion approved during 2019. The SBA estimates that its programs supported almost 800,000 jobs in 2019. Each $1 million in SBA loans resulted in 3 to 3.5 new jobs, according to a recent academic study, and this effect is stronger when local credit conditions are tight.

Given the complex impact of Basel III requirements on SME financing and the central role that SMEs play in the economic development, policymakers should continue to evaluate the impacts of Basel III regulations on SME lending and put consistent effort to further support SME access to finance. Such effort can provide a risk-mitigating environment for SME financing. There can be measures such as introduction of an SME-specific loan program, development of a public loan guarantee scheme, and developing of an SME-focused rating system with addressing data gaps for SMEs.

The cases outlined in this report can help economies develop in Asia and the Pacific, with a focus on financial products, risk management, and monitoring methodologies and nonfinancial services for SMEs. These findings also suggest that countries around the world consider following the lead of the US and the Republic of Korea in establishing a public lending scheme to support small-business revenues and growth, using the Industrial Bank of Korea and the U.S. Small Business Administration as templates.

These two government institutions have a proven track record of enhancing SME access to financing in their respective countries, and their cases can be used by policymakers in developing member countries in Asia and the Pacific.

References

Asian Development Bank (ADB). 2015. *Asia Small and Medium-Sized Enterprise (SME) Finance Monitor 2014.* Manila. https://www.adb.org/publications/asia-sme-finance-monitor-2014.

Asian Development Bank Institute (ADBI). 2018. The Role of SMEs in Asia and their Difficulties in Accessing Finance. *Working Paper Series.* Tokyo.

Armstrong, C. 2014. The Moderating Influence of Financial Market Development on the Relationship Between Loan Guarantees for SMEs and Local Employment Rates. *Journal of Small Business Management.* 52 (1). pp. 126–140

Ayadi, R. 2005. *The New Basel Capital Accord and SME financing: SMEs and the New Rating Culture.* Centre for European Policy Studies. http://aei.pitt.edu/11441/1/1268.pdf.

Ayyagari, M., A. Demirgüç-Kunt, and V. Maksimovic. 2017. *SME Finance.* World Bank. Washington, DC.

Beck and Demirguc-Kunt. 2006. Small and medium-size enterprises: Access to finance as a growth constraint. Science Direct Journal of Banking and Finance. Volume 30. Issue 11. November 2006. pp. 2931–2943. https://www.sciencedirect.com/science/article/abs/pii/S0378426606000926.

Beck, Demirguc-Kunt, and Maksimovic. 2005. Financial and Legal Constraints to Growth: Does Firm Size Matter? Wiley Online Library. The Journal of Finance. Vol. LX, No.1. https://onlinelibrary.wiley.com/doi/full/10.1111/j.1540-6261.2005.00727.x.

Beck, T., L. F. Klapper, and J. C. Mendoza. 2008. *The Typology of Partial Credit Guarantee Funds Around the World.* Washington, DC: World Bank.

Brown, J. D. and J.S. Earle. 2017. Finance and Growth at the Firm Level: Evidence from SBA Loans. *The Journal of Finance.* 72 (3). pp. 1039–1080.

Calomiris, C. W. et al. 2017. How Collateral Laws Shape Lending and Sectoral Activity. *Journal of Financial Economics.* 123 (1). pp. 163–188.

Caruana, J. 2003. Consequences of Basel II for SMEs. Address by Jaime Caruana, Governor of the Bank of Spain and Chairman of the Basel Committee on Banking Supervision, to the European Parliament. Brussels. 10 July. https://www.bis.org/review/r030714d.pdf.

Cole, R.A. and T. Frost. 2018. The Role of Financial Reporting Quality in Worldwide Access to Credit. Available at SSRN 3292551.

Cole, R.A., A. Dietrich, and T. Frost. 2019. SME Credit Availability Around the World: Evidence from the World Bank's Enterprise Surveys. In Midwest Finance Association 2013 Annual Meeting Paper.

Cole, R.A. and T. Sokolyk. 2018. Debt Financing, Survival, and Growth of Start-Up Firms. *Journal of Corporate Finance.* 50 (June). pp. 609–625.

Congressional Research Service. 2019. *Small Business Administration: A Primer on Programs and Funding.* https://crsreports.congress.gov/product/pdf/RL/RL33243/93.

Cortes, B.S. 2010. Impact of Small Business Administration Lending on State-Level Economic Performance: A Panel Data Analysis. *The International Journal of Business and Finance Research.* 4 (3). pp. 55–65.

Craig, B. R., W. E. Jackson, and J. B. Thomson. 2007. Small Firm Finance, Credit Rationing, and the Impact of SBA–Guaranteed Lending on Local Economic Growth. *Journal of Small Business Management.* 45 (1). pp. 116–132.

____. 2009. The Economic Impact of the Small Business Administration's Intervention in the Small Firm Credit Market: A Review of the Research Literature. *Journal of Small Business Management.* 47 (1). pp. 221–231.

Diamond, D. 1984. Financial Intermediation and Delegated Monitoring. *Review of Economic Studies.* 51 (3). pp. 393–414.

Djankov, S., C. McLiesh, and A. Shleifer. 2007. Private Credit in 129 Countries. *Journal of Financial Economics.* 84 (2). pp. 299–329.

Federal Reserve. 2017. Report to the Congress on the Availability of Credit to Small Businesses. US.

Federal Reserve. 2022. Availability of Credit to Small Businesses. https://www.federalreserve.gov/publications/2022-october-availability-of-credit-to-small-businesses.htm.

Small Business Administration (SBA). 2009. Review of the Recovery Act's Impact on SBA Lending. Board of Governors of the Federal Reserve System. Washington, DC.

Financial Stability Board (FSB). 2019. Evaluation of the Effects of Financial Regulatory Reforms on Small And Medium-Sized Enterprise (SME) Financing. The Financial Stability Board. November 2019. Basel.

Gozzi, J. C. and S. Schmukler. 2016. Public Credit Guarantees and Access to Finance. *Warwick Economics Research Paper* No. 2068–2018–1284. Warwick, UK.

Industrial Bank of Korea (IBK). 2014. *SME Financing and Role of Industrial Bank of Korea*. Seoul.

——. 2016. New Future in Finance for SMEs (2016). PowerPoint document. Seoul.

——. 2015~2019. IBK Fact Book. Seoul.

Armstrong, C2018~2019. Annual Report. Seoul.

——. 2020. IBK Internal Data. Seoul.

——. 2022. Industrial Bank of Korea Annual Report 2021. Seoul. https://vpr.hkma.gov.hk/statics/assets/doc/100291/ar_21/ar_21_eng.pdf.

Industrial Bank of Korea (IBK) Economic Research Institute. 2014. The Effect Analysis of the Win-Win Collaboration Loan.

Kobe, K., and R. Schwinn. 2018. Small Business GDP 1998–2014. SBA Office of Advocacy. Washington, DC.

Korea Development Institute (KDI). 2011. 2010. Modularization of Korea's Development Experience: SME Financing, KDI Knowledge Sharing Program.

Koo, J.H. and S.K. Kim. 2019. The evaluation of performance and value of the corporate restructuring system in 2019, Korea Institute of Finance's policy research paper to PRISM. http://www.prism.go.kr/.

Kuntchev, V. et al. 2012. What Have We Learned from the Enterprise Surveys Regarding Access to Finance by SMEs? Enterprise Analysis Unit of the Finance and Private Sector Development, World Bank. Washington, DC.

Kyong, R.S., D. Herrera, and A. Calatayud. 2015. Lessons for Latin America and the Caribbean from Korean Experiences in Productive Development. Inter-American Development Bank Working paper. Washington, DC.

La Porta, R. and A. Shleifer. 2014. Informality and Development. *Journal of Economic Perspectives*. 28 (3). pp. 109–126.

Organisation for Economic Co-operation and Development (OECD). 2017. *Financial Education for Micro, Small, and Medium-sized Enterprises in Asia*. Paris. https://www.oecd.org/finance/Financial-education-for-MSMEs-in-Asia.pdf.

Orzechowski, P.E. 2019. US Small Business Administration Loans and US State-Level Employment. *Journal of Economics and Finance*. pp. 1–20.

Padgett, S. 2013. The Negative Impact of Basel III on Small Business Financing. *Ohio State Entrepreneurial Business Law Journal*. 8 (1), pp. 183-207.

Roszbach, T. J. J. L. K. 2005. Credit Risk versus Capital Requirements under Basel II: Are SME Loans and Retail Credit Really Different? https://www.bis.org/bcbs/events/crcp05jacobson.pdf.

Social Security Administration. 2009. American Recovery and Reinvestment Act Helps Small Businesses. Washington, DC.

Stiglitz, R. and A. Weiss. 1981. Credit Rationing in Markets with Imperfect Information. *American Economic Review*. 71 (3). pp. 393–410.

United Nations Conference on Trade and Development (UNCTAD). 2002. *Improving the Competitiveness of SMEs in Developing Countries: The Role of Finance To Enhance Enterprise Development*. Geneva. https://unctad.org/system/files/official-document/itetebmisc3_en.pdf.

United Nations Economic and Social Commission for Asia and the Pacific (UNESCAP). 2004. Bulletin on Asia-Pacific Perspectives 2003/04. Bangkok. https://www.unescap.org/sites/default/d8files/bulletin03-04-ch7.pdf.

U.S. Small Business Administration (SBA). 2017. SBA Strategic Plan: Fiscal Year 2018–2022. Washington, DC.

____. 2018. Frequently Asked Questions. Office of Advocacy. Washington, DC. https://www.sba.gov/sites/default/files/advocacy/Frequently-Asked-Questions-Small-Business-2018.pdf.

____. 2019. 2019 Small Business Profile. Office of Advocacy. Washington, DC.

____. 2020a. Performance Plan, Budget, and Report, FY 2019 Annual Performance Report. SBA. https://advocacy.sba.gov/about/performance/

____. 2020b. Economic Bulletin. Office of Advocacy. Economic Bulletin (April). Washington, DC.

____. 2020c. Disaster Assistance Update Nationwide EIDL Loans. https://www.sba.gov/document/report-covid-19-eidl-loans-report-9-14-20.

World Bank. n.d. Small and Medium Enterprises (SMEs) Finance. Washington, DC. https://www.worldbank.org/en/topic/smefinance.

____. 1998. Ch. 8: Issues in informal finance. *World Development Report*. Washington, DC. Oxford University Press.

_____. 2017. *MSME Finance Gap: Assessment of the Shortfalls and Opportunities in Financing Micro, Small and Medium Enterprises in Emerging Markets*. Washington, DC.

World Bank. 2018. *Investigating the Financial Capabilities of SMEs: Lessons from a 24-Country Survey*. Washington, DC: World Bank. https://openknowledge.worldbank.org/entities/publication/60ee7c5b-9ef6-5f64-bff5-04c07dcd3475.

World Trade Organization (WTO). 2016. *World Trade Report 2016. Levelling the Trading Field for SMEs*. Geneva. https://www.wto.org/english/res_e/booksp_e/world_trade_report16_e.pdf.

www.ingramcontent.com/pod-product-compliance
Lightning Source LLC
LaVergne TN
LVHW071453180726
843512LV00018B/1366